Buried Alive

A story of hate and acceptance

by A. James

Buried Alive: A story of hate and acceptance
by Alex James

© 2020 Alex James

Published by Alex James: *alexjamesincorporated@gmail.com*

ISBN 978-0-473-52162-2

Disclaimer:

Alex James is not a therapist or a psychologist. The opinions expressed are his, based on his interpretation of existing research and his observations. The statistics cited in this book were sourced by the author from various dependable organisations between the months of September and December 2019, and were accurate when accessed.

CONTENTS

CHAPTER ONE

Hate and Acceptance

EIGHT HUNDRED THOUSAND people commit suicide every year; that's one friend, family member, mother, father, possibly someone close to you, every forty seconds. One human being every forty seconds, gone.

Someone who has experienced sexual abuse is three times as likely to be one of those people. One in five women and one in six men will be sexually abused before they turn twenty-five. For those of us who are survivors, the likelihood of one of us tragically checking out early is dramatically greater than for the general populace – and only increases with age. This is not a book about suicide; but suicide, mental illness, addiction and self-harm are all very possible realities for people who have experienced or are currently undergoing sexual abuse, at any time in their lives.

My name is Alex; I was sexually abused by my stepfather. Abused in one of the most abhorrent ways possible by the man who I trusted to act as a parental figure, the man who was supposed to protect me, guide me and show me how to be a man myself as I grew up. I hate him for that – I hate him, and everyone like him. People like him who inflict this harm on anyone deserve our hate.

My intention in writing this book is multifaceted. I want to tell my story, and I want that to be an example to others to tell theirs. I want survivors to know that it's safe to talk about their abuse – that there are people who will listen and support them. I believe that every honest conversation about sexual abuse and its impact makes the world a safer place for us all. I want to combat abusers and prevent further harm to victims. I feel the most effective and expedient way that we can fight back against this scourge is simply to talk about it. Your voice can help bring about change.

I thought long and hard about the best way to tell my story. I wanted to reach as many people as possible. Part of me wanted to get hold of a megaphone and yell my story at anyone within earshot, but I thought that may land me in some form of asylum where I would have only a limited and very captive audience. So, in light of that, I decided to undertake the sensible but daunting task of writing this book. *Buried Alive: A story of hate and acceptance* is my best attempt at an honest and complete account of my story of abuse, though to protect people's privacy I have awarded them new names for the purposes of my story.

If even one person who reads this book is inspired to come forward about his or her abuse, feels more confident about supporting someone else, or simply just becomes aware of the issues facing victims of sexual abuse, then I have succeeded. But before I can talk about any kind of success, I must first tell you my tale. And, like any sane person, I am going to start somewhere in the middle.

I was cold and numb as I drove home from work – strange, as it was a beautifully warm summer's day. A scenic view of the ocean passed me by almost unnoticed as I made my way toward my home on the Kāpiti Coast where I lived with my fiancée, Thea, in our jointly owned house only a short drive from the beach, with our menagerie of pets. I worked for a company that I believed in, doing a job that I enjoyed; not only was the work rewarding but it paid well too. I had finished around midday and the sun was high in the sky, creating a picturesque view out in the harbour; a stunning contrast between that and the rolling hills along the other side of the road. I could feel that sun on my skin through the windscreen and I had the windows down, listening to my favourite music.

But despite all this lovely scene setting I am cold, dead inside. I want to enjoy this moment in time and the next, but I am unable to. The few occasions where I have felt happiness have been fleeting and brief, brief escapes from the numbness I have grown familiar with, oozing over me like something from a vile pustule. I have no control over these feelings – I want them to release me, but I can't escape, and at this stage in my story I have not yet accepted my past. This utter lack of joy makes me feel ungrateful for what I have – I know that I'm lucky, but I'm unable to appreciate it ... Instead I feel disgusted with myself, and my subconscious thoughts remind me of this in every unoccupied quiet moment. A cacophony of judgmental voices screams at me at every opportunity: "Think of everyone else who has less" – "You haven't got it that bad" – "You don't deserve what you have" – "You worthless, ungrateful piece of shit" – "If you can't sort yourself out, why don't you just end it? No one wants to know you like this anyway" – "Drive your car into oncoming traffic and be done with it". Please, forgive my self-indulgence... but let me make something clear; I know I am fortunate, and I want more than anything to love my life. I don't want these thoughts, they aren't mine, but they fill my mind and I have begun to believe what they're telling me.

These thoughts are not my own, yet they have been with me since I was about 14 years old. At first they were dull and quiet, visiting only in the depths of night when sleep eluded me. They were loudest when I found myself staring into the void at night waiting for him to visit. As I have aged and become more aware of the grotesqueness of his crimes against me, they have become more persistent and inexplicably furious. They are perpetual, yet entirely unwelcome, guests. "He didn't mean to hurt you," they cry out to me; softly they whisper to me, "He loves you", "He's unwell – or was. He's better now...he wouldn't hurt anyone else." "Think of the hurt you would cause your family if you said anything – if you tell them it just shows how selfish you are," they urge, and then escalate with added venom, "You should be grateful for what you have, you ungrateful piece of shit – just die." Clearly, as you are reading what I have written, I did not succumb to the pressure from these thoughts, although at times they were terribly persuasive.

This particular drive, unlike many others I endured in similar fashion, was the catalyst for me to seek counselling for the first time – but the motivation wasn't internal. As you can imagine, a person in my state is not much fun to be around; in fact, I imagine that when I was at my lowest I was deeply upsetting to be near. Despite not yet knowing any of my story, Thea was deeply concerned for me, having observed a steady decline in my mood over the prior months. She firmly encouraged me to talk to someone – if not her, then someone else who could help me work through what I was experiencing. But at this point I had not yet told a living soul my story, and I by no means sprang into action arranging meetings with psychiatrists or counsellors or anything of the sort. I will spare you a description of the following days languishing in depression (I feel that would be too self-indulgent). So we will fast forward a few days: I am standing in the corridor at work, trying to subtly retrieve the number from a poster for a counselling service funded by my employer. For some reason I am embarrassed... "There's nothing wrong with me, is there?"

Fortunately for me, my prior history included an obsession with avenues of self-improvement. I had managed to convince myself that my unhappiness was somehow derived from some kind of skill or trait that I was lacking, and so on that particular day I had been listening to a podcast on taking action: "Only you are standing in the way of your own progress; it's up to you to take action!" Very corny, somewhat unhelpful self-help blather – however, in that moment it was exactly what I needed to hear. I was standing in the corridor, staring at that poster with the podcast host's voice shouting confidently: "Take action! Action!" Almost in direct reply my unwelcome visitors screamed out in protest: "There's nothing wrong with you! You don't need help, you ungrateful piece of shit! What would you even talk about? Think of all the pain you will cause!" And then – quite unexpectedly – I reached into my pocket, produced my phone and typed in the number for the counselling service. I left the office, the whole while staring at my phone. Down the stairs I went and into the car park. I got into my car, an early nineties Mitsubishi Mirage with frayed seats, and there, in that quiet moment of solitude, distracted by the fluorescent glow of the phone screen, I dialled that number.

Whilst so much more time would pass before I reached any kind of resolution or closure, that phone call set into motion the events that ultimately led me to where I am now on my journey of recovery. But before I reveal how that happened I need to tell you much more of my story.

So now you know where my journey to recovery and journey to acceptance started. But why start my story here? A perfectly reasonable question. When I decided to seek justice for myself, one of the first things I did was to seek out books of other survivors' experiences. There are many great books out there, but it was hard for me to read them. Many started with tales of abuse, and of course such accounts are important; we must talk about what happened to us in order to move past it. But for me, in the head space I was in at that time, I needed to be told it could get better. After reading this first chapter, you know it can get better, because I am telling you that it did for me. As I sit here writing these words, I have accepted my story and consider the matter of the abuse I suffered resolved. It is hard, don't let me lull you into a false sense of security. There aren't words in the English language capable of describing how arduous a journey you will be embarking on. But we are the sum of the trials we face in life; the anguish we feel in the face of adversity can act as fuel to get us through those miseries and see us emerge secure in ourselves and stronger than before.

The journey of recovery is not an easy one. Unlike many journeys you will take, this one doesn't have an end, per se. Does that seem to contradict what I just told you about things getting better? Perhaps if I didn't elaborate it would. The journey of recovery never truly ends; we must all accept what has happened to us as part of our story and acknowledge it without letting it define us. That doesn't mean you have to be okay with it. It is okay to feel anger for the suffering you endured during that part of your life; just understand that that part of your life is over now, and what you do with the rest is up to you. You can choose to continue languishing, as I did for so long, or you can choose to move past it and do something positive. Anger is an emotion that we all feel – it alerts us to injustices, and if used constructively it can help us see those wounds that spawned it be healed. I still hate my abuser for what he did to me, but I no longer allow him to flood the dark recesses of my mind. I have accepted that chapter of my life – it is in my timeline, but I am not ashamed of it. I speak freely of it and wield it as a weapon to fight the very same injustices that were done to me. The sexual abuse I suffered does not define me.

My story takes a while to tell, with much of it being overshadowed by the demons of my abuse. Those demons stole precious time which I will never be able to retrieve. As I struggled to come to terms with my abuse, a concept that helped me greatly was to think of my time as currency, a very limited and precious currency. I would encourage you to do the same. When you were abused, someone else took control of your currency and influenced how you invested it later in life (in my experience, through depression). I would see you seize back control of your time from your demons, depression, anxiety and fear. I want you to read my story and feel encouraged to take hold of the reins, either for yourself or to help someone you love, and start spending that currency the way that you want; it is finite, and once it's spent, whether you are happy with your purchases or not, your time is up.

So, you've picked up this book, you've read a few pages and you know some of my story. An ugly part, right around the middle of my journey. You know that things got better for me. You've read my clumsy analogy of time as a currency. You know that my journey to recovery hasn't finished and likely never will, but the sailing is a lot smoother now. But I didn't get here alone. Now you're thinking, "Well great – where's the advice?" To that I say, I have given you some indirectly: you will need support, and likely lots of it. It is okay to falter, and this journey is more than worthwhile; moreover, it may be the most important and self-defining thing you ever do. There's more coming, don't worry – but first I need to tell you my tale.

My abuse did not start immediately, I was not born into it. In fact, full-blown sexual abuse didn't start until I was fourteen years old. Did this make it any easier to deal with? No. But, because of this I have quite a lot to fill you in on, so let's get to it.

CHAPTER TWO

Earliest Memories

AS A YOUNG boy I used to visit my Aunt Karen frequently; I vaguely remember walking between her nearby house and mine. I must have been four years old when she escorted me home that day – the first day I met him. An odd yellow hue surrounds all the images I can recall, the fog of time I suppose. I remember being walked into the living room where the TV was on, I think it was *Snow White and the Seven Dwarves* playing. What sticks out in my memory the most was the figure standing in our kitchen. I seldom went in the kitchen at that house, except to be placed on the counter and given medicine. It was a very small rectangular room directly opposite the stairs, looking out into the garden.

In that small room, on this particular day, a black, seemingly motionless figure was staring out into the garden. I remember noticing the figure as I came into the room but paying it no heed initially until I sat down, when it moved directly into my field of view. I kept looking to my mother for explanation, but I don't remember articulating my concern – I feel as if I simply expected an explanation or introduction. As I recall, my aunt left soon after dropping me home.

I remember feeling many different things at this point. Had we recently come into possession of a statue? If so, what an odd place for it! Was this an intruder, perhaps? Should I be scared? I didn't know... I'd still been given no clue how to feel in this situation. *Snow White and the Seven Dwarves* was still playing, and I remember watching that and nothing further from that day. That was the first time I met him, the man who would become my stepfather and my tormenter. One day, in the near future, we would end up in the living room again.

Much of my memory from then on until some years later is hazy and fleeting at best, given my young age. More properly formed impressions come from the period after we had moved into military housing – he was in the Army, you see. I knew that much about him, and that his name was Ernest. I also knew he and my Mum were married – apparently I was their ring bearer, although I couldn't tell you a single thing about the wedding. I think they may have honeymooned in Cornwall, not that it matters. It's always seemed odd to me that I can remember the day I met him so vividly given my age, yet my parents' wedding is completely lost to me.

Our military housing, a small semi-detached house, was in Aldershot, the location of a large Army camp in the UK. It's in that house that the earliest event I would recount to police years later took place. Was it awful or harrowing? No, not really. But years later, reflecting on it puts my hair on end. I remember one evening, aged seven, lying absolutely terrified in my dark room and thinking to myself, "Come on, you're seven now, practically grown up!", whilst trying to talk myself out of a panic.

For no clear reason that I can recall, I decided to strike out on my own – run away from home. It's possible my step-father's furious temper was a motivation. It used to terrify me; at some point whilst living in Aldershot I did something to upset him and was consequently put into a large mail sack, thrown in the boot of his car and driven around for an unknown period. Was this a common occurrence? No, but it may have been a contributing factor to my decision here, who knows. I digress; on the evening of my departure I put on my Action Man dress-up outfit, grabbed a fabric tote bag that was in my room, loaded up a couple of toys and the large tub of raisins I was allowed for snacks, and set out to make my way on my own. It was roughly five o'clock in the evening at that point, summertime in the UK and the sun was still up; but nevertheless, off I went!

Where would I go? I knew exactly where I was going! To the large tree I would frequently play in that grew over the car park to the back of our house; that's where I would live out my days. The tree grew from someone else's back garden, but it was a big tree and kids were perpetually climbing into it, and I got the impression that the people occupying the house couldn't care less. That was especially clear on this occasion; they were looking directly at me from what I think was their kitchen window as I made my ascent towards my new life in the tree. Up I went, invisible to them of course, garbed as I was in my Action Man outfit. I climbed to a comfortable height and stopped, hung my worldly possessions from a reachable branch and decided to have my dinner – a clump of raisins. I stayed there for a bit, played with the toys I had decided to share this intrepid adventure with, ate a few more raisins, and slowly started to realise that trees are not comfortable places for long periods of time. Then I began to need the toilet and a slight chill invaded the air as the evening was setting in, though the sun was still very much up. By now I felt hours had past, but since it was still light and my observers (now sharing a hot beverage) were still looking on, it could only have been forty-five minutes at the very most. I was also terrified of the dark and didn't own a torch or know where my parents kept theirs to pilfer it before I departed forever – thoughts which only crept into my head as I made my way back down the tree. Perhaps it was best that I head home and try again another day.

I trundled home, tote bag in tow, where I was immediately accosted by my mother. I don't remember if it was a worried embrace, a stern telling-off, or both. But I do remember being told that he was out in his car looking for me, and I had best run upstairs and pretend to be asleep before he got home. (I can attest to his temper and imaginative punishments when I misbehaved.) The journey upstairs has been lost to the sands of time, but I am sure it was swift. The memory haze lifts again for me and I am in bed, doing my best sleeping impression – I may have even worked out by then that people breathe more slowly and deeply in their sleep (something I would become adept at simulating later in life), so I am sure that I was giving a stellar performance. I had heard him arrive home along with some mumbling near the front door, most likely an explanation that I had also returned home. Up the stairs he came and into my room. Then something strange happened: he stood there a distance from my cabin bed, where I slept elevated at about head height for an average adult. Then he reached out and stroked me. He withdrew his arm once he had traced my body from head toe, then he would reach out once more, starting from my head, down to my toes. He did this several times, head to toe, like you might stroke a cat sitting on your lap in the evening. At the time I thought nothing of this whatsoever – I counted myself lucky to be escaping a hiding, and hoped that my pretend sleeping was convincing. My only complaint was that his hands were cold. But sitting here now, writing and reflecting on that moment in time, I find myself wanting to throw up. Although I consider myself to have closure, the events of my abuse still have an effect on me – the difference being that now I am not afraid to talk about them. But I digress. If I had known what I do now about the man standing in front of me that night, I would never have come down from that tree.

We continued living in that house for a while longer; postings in the UK Military are quite short, generally two years, so we would be on the move again shortly. In the time that remained, I was a happy kid. We would visit Bird World some weekends, a nearby avian wildlife park. I would make friends, fall out with them and make up again, as children do. I learnt to ride a bike in the same car park from which I would climb into that tree, and I would ride that bike to the local spa shop or Naafi (Navy, Army and Air Force Institutes), as we would refer to it sometimes. Occasionally on weekends my biological father would come and pick me up and I'd spend days with him in his flat in London, which I remember being great fun. I remember exploring the city with him and eating new foods, learning how to use tools and then building something with them. Or visiting relatives in faraway towns, and sometimes spending half-terms there. I loved spending time with my father. I remember my Dad introducing me to the lady he would eventually marry and who would become my stepmother. That was a very confusing period of time for me, not because I was upset about my Dad meeting someone (although I understand that can be a normal thing for children to experience) but because I just had no idea what was happening.

My immediate family at this point in the story consisted of myself, Mum, my stepfather, my Dad and my stepmother to be. I did not and still don't fully understand the circumstances of my biological parents' relationship or why they separated – or if they were ever together. When I became aware my Dad was in a relationship with another woman, I found this very disturbing. Was this normal? Do mums and dads do that? Of course they do... my Mum and stepfather live together... don't they? It was all a bit much for my young mind to comprehend without explanation. I never asked for any, or if I did it was never given. But because of this I remember struggling with all aspects of my family dynamics from that time on. I would return home to Aldershot confused, and back to my Dad's again some point in the future befuddled – and so on it went. But I must record that I have no ill feelings towards my stepmother, a wonderful lady who always showed me love and kindness.

Soon Ernest and my Mum's first child would arrive, my brother. I remember that being a bit of fun! That is about all I remember though; I don't think it's the type of thing that is important to a young boy. Another brother would arrive within the next two years. My brothers, whilst important to me, are not hugely pivotal to the tale I am telling and now live their own private lives, and so will only feature where pertinent.

Soon after the arrival of my first brother we moved to a Military house in Yateley. Moving at this age (about eight or nine years old) is always a hard thing, leaving all one's friends in the local area behind. But I was fortunate: part of the agreement my mother and father had was that my father would pay for my education. I was attending Lyndhurst Primary School in Camberley, where I had a large group of great friends – and even though we had moved, I was able to keep going there and seeing my "school friends" regularly. At the time it meant everything to me; each time we moved house I found it absolutely heart wrenching to have to leave a friend group behind, and at such a young age I had not yet had to endure any emotional torment that would numb me to such things. Having a stable group of school friends was truly a saving grace.

The headmaster and mistress of this school were significant role models for me. The headmaster was a firm but fair man who commanded respect wherever he went (in the school, anyway); he would address all of us first thing in the morning and impart life lessons before joining us in hymns. He was always well dressed and polite, and seldom did his temper boil over; yet we were all terrified of angering him. The headmistress was a similar character, but far more involved in the day-to-day activities of the school; she would frequently join us for lunch and helped run many of the after-school activities, including being the Cub leader for our

Cub group. I learnt a lot through the medium of Cubs: life skills like cooking, cleaning, socialising and other tasks that become critical when one reaches a point of independence.

So we were still in the Yateley house, and school was still in Camberley. I enjoyed school, I got into trouble a good percentage of the time, my parents were called in a lot, my teachers continued to discipline me fairly. I must say, reflecting on that time, that I had no complaints about how life was going. And aside from my stepfather's irregular behaviour when we first met and when I decided that running away and starting my own life might not be for me, I can't think of any early warning signs to alert me about what was to come.

Whilst we lived at the Yateley house, my godfather Anthony started taking me to Sunday morning hockey. I loved visiting my Dad, but Anthony was a huge part of my life and he was always great to me. He would always spoil me when he took me out, and when I visited his house he would try and get me to watch football. Though I wouldn't be interested, and instead of partaking in the activity he wanted to share with me I would beg to watch cartoons, he still loved me. He was invested in me and my development for some reason; perhaps he saw I lacked a full-time male role model? Maybe he sensed something off about Ernest and wanted to be close to me to make sure I was protected? I don't know. So, hockey: like all new things I was awful at first, but soon learnt the basics and steadily improved. At times I would even be confident enough to say that I was good. This is one of the few childhood activities I could draw confidence from. I was awful at most sports, but that didn't bother me now because I was good at hockey. Anthony would pick me up every Sunday and take me to practice and drive me to every away game we played. At the time I didn't grasp what a huge demand on his time this must have been. I will always be thankful for that time, the irretrievable currency he invested in me.

Sunday morning sports – a trivial note in the story of life; but if you can't identify anything in your life that gives you confidence, that will spill over into everything you do. I might not have been good at football, but I'd give it a go. If I sucked, I was still good at hockey. That school play I was terrified to perform in, I'd give it a shot – if I made a fool of myself, that was alright, I was still good at this other thing. Being good at something gave me the confidence to branch out and try other things; to reference the English poet William Cowper – possibly not entirely accurately – "variety's the very spice of life". I have my uncle Anthony to thank for that confidence and all the positive, happy memories that came as a result. Without the support and lessons he taught me early on in life, I would likely not be here today.

The story develops and darkens as we go further, but my life was not awful growing up. It was not all confusion and chaos culminating in tragedy; I had friends, structure, things I looked forward to. I also felt loved by my family. I was abused, but my life prior to those events was not an indicator of or a precursor to my abuse. I had people who cared about me deeply and were looking out for me, guardians and carers. I had almost a separate family in my Dad and stepmother. I could have run to them for help, but I was not armed with the skills to talk about my feelings or close personal experiences, and later events isolated me from my

Dad. Like Sunday morning hockey, emotional intelligence and the ability to talk freely about uncomfortable topics are things that must be learnt and practised, because most of us don't come out well versed in those skills. We are all potential victims; terrible fates can befall us at any time, and there is almost no way to prepare for them when and if they do. But you can hone your ability to talk. If I had talked about what happened to me in the beginning, I could have saved myself harrowing trauma over many years and my family from a rupture that would shake them to the foundations and change their lives forever. Talking about our experiences is the best way not only to combat those abusers who hide in plain sight, but also to protect our loved ones from the devastation our abusers will otherwise wreak.

Between the period of Aldershot and Yateley my Aunt Karen passed away from cancer. We attended the funeral and visited her grave frequently, yet we seldom discussed her passing or the effect that it had on us. Remember that emotional intelligence I was talking about before? We just didn't have it. As a family we didn't discuss uncomfortable topics – on the contrary, we preferred to actively avoid them. If as a family we had engaged in more real topics, the trajectory of our lives might have been so different. That's not to say that I would have condemned my family to suffer additional tribulations in order to provide material for tough conversations so that we could become better at sharing our feelings or adept at navigating complex situations. I simply wish that, as a child, the troubles we did experience were better explained to me, so I better understood my own emotions rather than being confused by them.

Explaining emotionally or morally difficult situations to a child can be incredibly challenging. It is very easy for me to sit here, in the comfort of my armchair, and preach that it is a practice that must be carried out, or complain that I wasn't guided through such situations with as much finesse as I would have liked. Yet regardless of how arduous the task is, it is necessary. Children are not born with an innate ability to comprehend such situations; as with many things, their understanding must be taught and developed over time. I am not suggesting that dinner time topics be changed from the details of the day to sessions on the works of Kant, or that bedtime stories be replaced with readings of Nietzsche. But when situations that may be morally or emotionally ambiguous to a child *do* arise, talk your child through the situations, listen to what they have to say, and encourage them to express their feelings. By helping a child better understand situations and their associated feelings, you are helping that child build coping mechanisms and a deeper sense of self. Retelling the event in the form of a story can be an excellent way to help a child rationalise it. Storytelling engages not only the analytical side of the brain but also the emotional side.

So how does the efficacy of storytelling pertain to a story of sexual abuse? If you were to ask a select group of primary school-aged children if they would take candy from a stranger, I guarantee the majority of them would say no and that they would flee the stranger to seek help. This is because they have been told some form of the age-old story where a child is offered candy by a stranger, and is consequently kidnapped. That story develops a mental model that will influence a child's actions if he or she is presented with that situation. Telling children that story has helped our society protect them from the dangers of child abduction. Yet most of us aren't warning our children, through the medium of storytelling, about strangers who would seek to sexually abuse them – even though an unfortunate and harsh reality is that a lot more children are molested than kidnapped, at least in the developed world. The stories don't have to be graphic; simply telling a child that if anyone tries to touch them inappropriately or take photos of them then they should flee and find an adult is enough to start building those mental models, the first line of defence against would-be abusers.

* * * * *

I hope I haven't lost you to a mundane and incomplete retelling of my early years, and a short anecdote about the power of storytelling in protecting children. It was important to me to show you that for the most part I had a normal happy upbringing. The story soon becomes more condensed. As an adult reflecting on the next part of my childhood, I begin to see the points where my stepfather started putting his claws into my life, isolating me and assuming more control over me. It was done in such a way that no one would notice – I certainly didn't see it coming. How did this predator succeed? With camouflage, under the guise of being a doting stepparent.

CHAPTER THREE

Prototypical

LIKE MANY MIDDLE-CLASS people (the ones that I've met, anyway) my parents aspired to purchase their own property; a piece of the world to declare their own. I suppose the appeal of paying your own mortgage instead of someone else's is a strong one. A momentous task, nonetheless, only made more daunting with children in tow. My understanding is that parents often help their children when it comes time to purchase their first house, and the case was no different here. As it happened, my grandmother owned the house my parents wanted, so they were able to purchase it from her at a reasonable price, with financial assistance from my step-grandfather. We were moving away from the Yateley house, leaving another friend group behind and beginning a new chapter. Living the dream? Funnily enough, this was the house where I first met my stepfather Ernest in the previous chapter. I don't know who owned it then, but it was certainly my grandmother's before my parents acquired it.

Sandhurst is where we ended up – and what a great place that was! My room was small, but I had no complaints; I prefer smaller rooms. Something about larger ones made me uneasy, especially at night. As my parents owned the place this was the first time I was able to paint my room a colour other than white! I so desperately wanted the whole room red, but Mum convinced me that blue was a more reasonable colour. She was probably right ... she also managed to convince me that painting only half the room would make it look bigger ... To this day I disagree, but it's all semantics now. The house was semi-detached in a large suburban development with a park in the centre which made for lovely walks. Our house had a gate that allowed you to access the forest directly through the back garden; I made good use of it. I made new friends; one kid in particular, Rob, lived just on the corner of our street. Sandhurst was also very close to Camberley, so getting to school was even quicker now!

The years passed and all was well. At the age of ten going on eleven, I was coming to the end of my time at Lyndhurst, and I had begun perusing secondary schools to attend. Given my Dad was paying for my education, I was looking primarily at private schools with entrance exams you needed to pass before you would be considered. Though I had been a troublesome pupil I enjoyed school, and by this point had begun to outgrow a lot of my boyish tendencies, so was able to apply myself. I sat several entrance examinations for many schools I wanted to attend – Salesian College in Farnborough in particular, where I was desperate to go. Can I remember exactly why? Like many things back then, no. Going into that examination I was petrified – I wanted to pass so badly. I had sat tests before through primary school, but this was the first proper test where if I "failed" I would be denied something I wanted ... Yes, I had all that "hockey confidence" – but damnit, if I didn't pass this test, I would have to go to some random school I would hate! Or so I convinced myself. I sat that test, palms sweaty, I did my best, went home and waited. After a few weeks of waiting, I got the letter from Salesian; I had aced the entrance exam and was offered a place to attend school there.

My relationship with my godfather, my Uncle Anthony, started to change a little after the move to Sandhurst, especially after sitting my entrance exams. I felt very grown up and would much rather hang out with friends now than see family. We would still see him, and he would still come up to take me to sports – but the sport changed from field hockey to roller hockey due to our new location. Practices for this sport were less frequent, and to be honest I didn't enjoy them as much. I believe he wanted me to keep going and spend time with me; but my unwillingness to participate, and/or lack of enthusiasm for roller hockey compared to field hockey, likely made the long trip he had to make to pick me up seem less worthwhile. Although the man was great to me, I loved him, and I have no doubt it was reciprocated, unfortunately I began seeing significantly less of him around this time. Consequently I became separated from my main male role model and father figure.

Despite the dwindling influence of my Uncle Anthony in my life, I continued to enjoy my time in Sandhurst. I got to hang out with friends in the evening and a whole new group at school. Not only that, I was also still very proud of myself for passing my entrance exam to Salesian. One evening before the end of the school year, I recall being in my room when my Mum paid me a visit. She was visibly agitated, shoulders slumped forward and tense. The lights weren't on in my room and the curtains were pulled to keep the heat in, making it so dark I couldn't see her eyes, which only added to the vexed and uneasy feelings stirring in me at her unusual appearance. I would like to quote what she said directly, but since I don't possess perfect recall you will need to accept my paraphrasing. What she told me was that she and my Dad had fallen out; he would no longer be paying for my schooling, and as a result I was no longer permitted to see him.

The time it took for her to impart that information took about the same amount of time as it did for you to read it: not long. I couldn't comprehend the news that I couldn't see my Dad any more. A rage-induced fury came over me; I threw things around my room. I was angry, frustrated and hurt. How was I to process this news? I couldn't. I just stayed there in my room and cried. I had never had a hard conversation with anyone, and this wasn't even a conversation, it was a horrible statement of fact communicated in a manner void of emotion. I was presented with that news and then left to accept it. I should have talked to someone about it, but I didn't know how. I should have expressed how I felt in some manner, but couldn't – not even creatively. My Dad and his whole family were now lost to me – how was I to process that? By now I had two other brothers, my Dad and stepmother having started their own family. Whilst I only had limited time with my brothers, I cared for them deeply, and the prospect of never seeing them again was a deep cut.

Writing this now, I still feel a twinge of sorrow and anger from that day. At the time, the thought that my stepfather may have had something to do with this, or that this might have been his first move to start separating me from the rest of my family, didn't even cross my mind. That concept seems a little clearer now.

Over the following days it dawned on me that now my father had been excluded from my life, there would be no money for schooling. No money for schooling meant no Salesian College. All those plans and ideas I had been sharing with my friends on the playground at school, gone. That hard work and triumph? Wasted. A whole new dimension was added to my bewilderment, made worse by my inability to express what I was feeling. It's a very British problem being so emotionally cut off.

So now when I finished at Lyndhurst I was to attend the local public school, Sandhurst College – and so I did. Was this the worst thing in the world? Of course not. Things could definitely have been much worse for me at this point, so please don't think less of me for rolling around in the metaphorical filth of self-pity. The plus side here was that some of the friends I had made locally were also going to be attending Sandhurst; how great was that! Including my friend Rob from around the corner.

By deciding, rapidly and unhealthily, to push the grief and hurt of losing my Dad deep down inside instead of talking about it and properly experiencing my emotional hurt, I was very quickly able to see this as a good turn of events. Sandhurst was the local secondary school, so I could ride my bike there with my friends, I could come home at lunch, and the days were shorter than those of most schools I had looked at previously! I had lost my father, but it was clear I could do nothing about that in my current position, and these other factors were all big positives in a kid's book when discussing school. When it comes to weighing up the pros and cons of education, anything that will allow more time for goofing off and having fun seems like a great idea.

I can put a concrete time stamp here: I was eleven years old and starting Year Seven at Sandhurst Secondary School. I say this confidently, as children start Year Seven, the first year of secondary school, at age eleven in the UK. For the most part, all was well! I had friends locally before starting and I made new friends whilst there. This school was a different world when compared to the upper-class education I was privileged to experience at Lyndhurst. Classes were scattered across the school, there was rubbish all over the place (which made for a great detention activity) I witnessed my first fist fight, got punched in the face myself, went on to get into some myself, learnt how to make rockets out of fizzy drink bottles and that kids smoked! This school was where I "belonged", socioeconomically speaking. Attending the primary school I did was a privilege enabled by my Dad's money.

Long story short, school was school. It was rough and I learnt a plethora of new life lessons, had some great times and learnt very little in terms of curricular education. One thing I did not learn was how to properly express myself. How would anyone even teach a preteen that? It's not really a teacher's place, is it? Is it something learned by happenstance through shared experience? I don't know. I now think it's a parent's responsibility to act as an example for their children so that they don't become shut off — so their children don't turn out like me. Perhaps I am getting unnecessarily deep here. I enjoyed that year. Trading Yu-Gi-Oh cards in the playground, hanging out in the fields after school ,and chucking rocks in frozen ponds trying to break the ice. I wouldn't have wanted to give all that up.

It was about this time that Ernest started coming into my room in the evenings before bed. Did this alarm me? Of course not – he used to read to me as a child, and would have been in the room after I fell asleep. I wasn't at all worried about this. At first he would just sit on my bed to read, then leave when I said I was going to sleep. As time went by, he would stay longer and longer and want to keep reading. One evening he nonchalantly lifted the covers whilst I was in bed and got in himself. He sat there for a while reading as if it was quite normal, then looked down at me and asked, "Is this ok?" I don't remember how I answered. You can be confident in your assumption: I did not breathe a word about this to anyone.

Our living room in Sandhurst was quite small, with an odd cupboard, quite large, at about chest height in the wall. Weird, right? My brothers and I would play in there all the time. The kitchen was off the living room, as I explained at the beginning, and that kitchen looked into the garden.

Something strange is happening now. My Mum is telling me that I have told her a kid at school threatened to stab me, and because of that we are going to sell the house. I will be going to a boarding school and my family will be moving back to Military housing. I am obviously paraphrasing again. Did I feel much at this time? Not really. I think emotions are a bit like muscles: if you don't use them, they simply waste away – and I certainly had no use for emotions. As a result, my feeble and useless emotions had all but rotted away. I would pretend in certain situations and act as I thought I should act, but generally felt nothing other than confusion at many points in my life. This was one of them. Emotionally confused but also genuinely confused. Had I told my Mum that a kid at school had threatened to stab me? To be honest with you, this type of thing was thrown around at school on an hourly basis – it was a rough school! It did shock me when I first turned up, but now, almost a year down the line, this kind of thing didn't faze me at all; kids threatened to stab each other all the time, but it never happened! If I did tell my Mum, I would have unthinkingly dropped it into conversation because I had become so desensitised to it, not because I was genuinely scared.

But back to the point at hand: we were on the move again. I may have protested this with my Mum, I may not have; I don't remember. What I remember is being mightily pissed off that we were leaving my friends behind again. But this time I was walking away from my school, which I had grown very accustomed to, without finishing the year. Perhaps I should have protested more than I did? But it was all so well packaged. Apparently I had given my parents cause for concern, and they were reacting appropriately. But were they? Why wasn't the school more involved here? If they had an attendee on their roster threatening to harm their law-abiding students with a knife, wouldn't they want to know so they could take action? What about the police? If you are about to give up your whole life wouldn't you at least want to dot some i's and cross some t's first?

These are things I would ask my Mum if I was able to revisit that moment in time, although, if time travel was real,

I wouldn't be writing this book. What I mean to say here is that I don't think these decisions were my Mum's, or were what she wanted. I strongly suspect – nay, believe – she was entirely influenced by my stepfather. I also believe that I was too. I believe that whatever I said or didn't say to my Mum about this miscellaneous school stabber was fabricated by my stepfather, and that this package deal she informed me that we were about to open was entirely prepared by him. Mothers under duress don't calmly calculate how to completely remove themselves from their lives and insert themselves somewhere else. It isn't human nature to run away at the slightest sign of danger, is it? Parents don't just accept that someone is trying to do harm to their children and move on with their lives. No, he had prepared all of it and manipulated my Mum into buying the crap he was selling. He had looked after me long enough, earned enough trust and invested enough of his own time – now he wanted his payday.

All the while that these events were unfolding, Ernest continued to visit my bedroom at night, slowly getting more and more comfortable. He was still getting into my bed to read and had even started staying there after I had fallen asleep; he was always gone when I woke up. I chose simply to ignore this behaviour and wrote it off as weird. It's embarrassing, right? A grown man coming into your room and sitting in your bed, under the covers. A teenage boy doesn't want to admit that something like that is happening to himself, let alone talk about it to anyone else! The night when I was given the news that we were packing up this life and going back to Military housing and I was getting sent off to

boarding school, he visited me. He came into my room before bed but didn't get in; he sat next to my bed this time. I
was laying on my front, upset and confused, going through
events in my head, and didn't much feel like seeing anyone,
let alone my odd stepfather with a wickedly short fuse who
had insisted on making a nightly routine of getting into my
bed. On this occasion though, as I said, he did not get into
my bed; he simply started rubbing my back as if to soothe
me. Perverse behaviour? Not really, you might even interpret
it as endearing and caring, a stepfather making an effort to
physically console his stepson in a time of distress. But he
had never done this before, never. At that isolated moment in
time, I don't think it would be fair to interpret the act of rubbing my back as inappropriate ... yet. If I didn't say anything
about him getting into my bed and reading, you can be sure
I didn't feel comfortable telling anyone when he rubbed my
back. Nor did I say anything when he kept coming back to
do it – but come back he did. Every night, it seemed, he came
back to my room, read, and then wanted to rub my back as I
feel asleep. Eventually he would want to rub my back in the
bed, sometimes without his shirt. He chose a time when he
knew I would be feeling defeated and vulnerable to establish this routine, this habit that would essentially normalise
his presence in my room at night. He planned out this entire
thing and it makes me sick; I hate him for it. I wish I had
said something, to someone, anyone. If nothing else, remember this; you can talk to someone. Anyone. You have that
option, if not someone you know personally, then there are
any number of anonymous services that can help you, set up
for this very purpose. I implore you, don't silence yourself

through misguided stoicism, embarrassment or fear. Speak and be heard, tell anyone who will listen, get help.

CHAPTER FOUR

Shadow of the Slasher

MY TIME AT Sandhurst Secondary School was up, the term was over, and I was now finishing the year at Licensed Victuallers School in Ascot, a private school educating both day students and boarders. Because we had sold the house in Sandhurst and moved into military accommodation at my behest (because of the phantom stabber), an Army allowance was available to us which subsidised my fee for attending such an establishment. Three cheers for private education. You may be able to guess – I felt pretty awful about this. My family has had to uproot their entire lives and move because of me? Not a good feeling for a teenager, I can tell you that much. Luckily, I had all of those emotions on lockdown, so apart from the initial guilt I didn't have too many lingering regrets attached to the move at the time.

You'll never guess where we ended up, though. Apparently we were a family that just loved doubling back on ourselves; we moved to Aldershot. Not to the same house, mind you – that might have been too much, especially as my brothers were both getting bigger now. But this house wasn't big either. My room in Sandhurst was small, but this one was even smaller. It fitted just my bed and a bedside cabinet, with no room for additional furniture or unwanted guests. The downstairs portion of the house was quite spacious and modern and the garden was nice, but the upstairs was small. Not just my room – the whole second storey was cramped and close; no one could be unaccounted for up there. Coincidently, Ernest did not visit me during the nights whilst we lived there. We weren't there long at all.

Now we need to talk about my boarding school, the other event happening around this time as a result of the knife-wielding lunatic whom it was apparently completely OK not to alert the authorities to. I was going on thirteen years old now, finishing Year Seven of secondary school. The boarders all gathered at the school the night before the term started, an event I would grow to look forward to, catching up with friends after holidays and the like. On this particular occasion, the first time I would show my face at this school, two thirds of the way through the year, it's safe to say I was not quite so enthusiastic. On the contrary, I believe I was apprehensive prior to the event. In light of that, though, my Mum had bought me a new outfit to wear to school and spoiled me a bit, so come the time to actually leave home, I think I was feeling quite good about the situation.

The introduction ended up being a complete breeze. Usually, all the kids from Year Seven and above got sent to Guinness boarding house for secondary school students. Unfortunately (or fortunately, depending on your stance), this year there had not been enough space in Guinness, so some Year Sevens stayed back in Bass house, the primary school boarding house. I want to acknowledge here that I don't think it's appropriate to name schoolhouses after brands of alcohol

– as a father myself, I would not want to send my child to a school almost openly promoting booze. However, the school was founded to support Licensed Victuallers and their families, a Licensed Victualler being an innkeeper who could sell alcohol. And at the time I didn't even give it a moment's thought or recognise half the names as anything other than schoolhouses.

As I was saying, some Year Sevens stayed back in Bass house; I was one of those. This meant that I only needed to initially introduce myself to a single dorm room of boys my age, not an entire boarding house of kids aged up to sixteen, a much more daunting prospect – especially so far through the school year. There were plenty of younger students in Bass, being the primary school house, but I felt no need to talk with any of them on that first night.

I genuinely do not remember my first classes at LVS (as it was and still is known), or even much of the remainder of my Year Seven schooling; likely the result of spending the better part of fifteen years repressing memories of my teenage years. I can't remember that school holiday, and I can't remember moving houses again; I have lost that entire segment of my memory. Perhaps it will return to me one day, as so much else has, but for now it has been rendered utterly blank.

We spent a year or less in that Aldershot house as a family, and then moved to a far larger house in Dorset. Ernest had been commissioned in the Army, and he received his promotion and was consequently posted there. Our new home had larger rooms on the second storey where we all slept, large enough to accommodate unwelcome visitors, and certainly large enough for people to go unaccounted for.

Year eight started. There were still space issues in the boarding houses; some of the group with whom I originally moved into Bass house have now been moved to Guinness. We were all envious, but were promised that as space was made available throughout the year we could all move over to be with our peers. The up side was that as Year Eights we were sharing an eight-man room between four of us – not a bad deal. But there were also less people close to me to notice a dramatic change in my persona.

Now we were in the much larger house, Ernest had resumed visiting my room. He started off slow, again, and would only visit to talk or read, sitting on my bed until I fell asleep – essentially repeating the pattern of behaviour he exhibited in Sandhurst. This time around I was far less troubled by it – I simply paid it no heed. I even stopped thinking that it was strange. It was my normal. You would be forgiven for thinking, at this point, "Aren't you safely tucked away at boarding school? How can this man still be a threat to you?" Weekends, my friends: at LVS it was customary for students to return home in the weekends. Some parents either couldn't accommodate that or perhaps couldn't be bothered showing up to collect their spawn for those two days, and those kids would stay, for the most part. You had to leave site for one weekend in four at least, this was the rule; even the international students were made to stay with their guardians during those weekends. But guess who never had a problem showing up to collect me? You guessed right: Ernest. He would be there on time every Friday night.

Ernest's manner also changed around the time we moved to Dorset, Wool specifically. He became far more personable and friendly towards me. As a younger child I had always been wary of him and afraid of his temper, but it seemed as if he had changed and was a calmer man now. This made me much less cautious around him – he seemed almost "cool" apart from the odd visits at night.

My Mum had always forbidden me to have a cell phone. I was actually gifted one once when I was younger, but she would not let me have a SIM card, so it was just a piece of plastic. She was worried about the implications of cancer, you see. Ernest didn't have an issue with me having a cell phone, he actually gave me one and if I broke it later on, he would go to great lengths to replace it very quickly. My Mum was convinced that this was necessary because I was living most of my time away from home and would need it to contact them. This seemed like the best thing ever for me! In reality, the people I had to talk to were right there in my dorm, for the most part, and cell phones were only allowed out during particular hours of the evening; Ernest was also the only person who would call or text me on it. It was actually a huge pain – reception was so poor that I had to walk to remote spots around the school to receive his call. The pay phones fixed to the wall in the common areas of the boarding house were far more convenient; all the other kids used them. This would mean conversation would be overheard by others, though. Like I said, he would call me on it almost nightly during the periods where we could use them, and talk to me for hours. He would text me as well, but he told me something strange about texting. He told me that other people could access my phone and read what we were saying, and that he would always sign his texts with a particular symbol so I would know it was him and that I shouldn't respond if he didn't use that symbol. How peculiar – but at the time I thought nothing of it. At this stage Ernest was not an abuser – he was an odd man, but my stepfather all the same, who had recently shown a different, friendlier side to his personality.

Even though I was becoming well practised at ignoring the nightly visits when I was home, they had become very tedious and awkward. Kids I had made friends with at school had also introduced me to the concept of online gaming, not something I could try at school because we didn't have internet, but a pastime I was very keen to dabble in when I got home. I also had a fondness for console games, so being able to play those on the internet with other people seemed amazing and otherworldly. One weekend, upon establishing that our dial-up connection was suitable for playing RuneScape, it dawned on me that I could entirely avoid Ernest if I just stayed up playing games all night. "Eureka!" I thought as I played into the small hours of the night in the study; I felt very clever. Of course, this activity was immediately admonished by my mother when she found out and that was the end of that. I could still play games, but bedtime was bedtime when I was home, unless I wanted to read. Ultimately video games would become my escape when I was home. I would avoid sleep for as long as possible so that I could delay his inevitable presence in my bed, doing what he would with me.

Fourteen years old is a pretty normal time for parents to have "The Talk" with their kids; some have it earlier, some have it later. I don't have any idea when I'll have the talk with my kids, thankfully that's a way off for me yet! Popular TV shows depict it as some awfully cringey interaction between stereotypically blank parents and their lively kids, ultimately resulting in the kids being repulsed whilst the parents still try and explain, telling them how "beautiful" or "normal" it is, and how everyone does it. *American Pie* takes a slightly ruder but more light-hearted and funny approach when Noah discovers his son Jim having sex with a pie, prompting the conversation later in the day. Probably the most iconic build up to "The Talk" ever. My talk was not even remotely similar to either of these versions. I'll elaborate further shortly, but first I must warn the reader: I am about to discuss the first time I was sexually abused by my stepfather.

CHAPTER FIVE

Fracturing

I HAVE TRIED as best I can to explain through story how I wound up here, what type of person Ernest was, how my family dynamics worked, and how he got his hooks in me. How he finally managed to facilitate full blown sexual abuse is a tougher topic to tackle. Tough to write, deeply upsetting to reread, a nightmare to have lived through.

It started the night my Mum sent him upstairs to my room to discuss "the birds and the bees" with me. I knew this was the intention behind the conversation before the fact, because Ernest had told me that Mum had asked him to and that we should have it in my room that evening. I was home from school for half term, a week off in the middle of the school term, which was good; it meant we could get this awkward conversation over and done with and quickly return to being our normal functioning uncommunicative and fairly emotionally cold family in the coming days. So there I sat, awaiting this conversation that I was apprehensive to have and was expecting to be immensely embarrassing given the TV I had watched and movies I had seen that touched on the matter. I was feeling vulnerable in anticipation of this uncomfortable conversation I was about to have with the man who had become more tolerable recently, and would get into my bed at night.

Autobiographical recollection is a hard thing for many survivors; the longer we wait to talk about our experiences, the harder it becomes. Certain details of that night are as clear as day, almost burned into my memory, and some are foggy and obscured at best. Every time I would discuss that night at therapy or retell the story, recollection would come a little easier. There's a chance that after this is written I may remember more. This is the most accurate account I have ever given of that first night he abused me.

I was waiting for him in my room in anticipation of an explanation of the dynamics of sex and how the male and female bodies interacted, a confusing topic for a young teenager. I was sitting on my single bed, which was pushed up into the corner of my room, maximizing the empty floor space. Even though I was in my early teens, my room still looked like it belonged to a young boy. I had Action Man curtains on my windows, drawers of toys and childish books on my shelves – signs of a room that isn't lived in much, which really didn't reflect me at all. I was sitting there thinking these things and anticipating the uncomfortable opening lines as he came into the room. He opened the door and shut it behind him; my lights weren't on, but the room was lit by a fading ambient light from outdoors as he approached my bed. He looked around as he entered, taking it in as if he didn't know the place, although he had been in here many times before at a similar hour of day. He still appeared to be adjusting to the room as he perched himself fervently on the bed next to me. I was still reluctantly awaiting those cringeworthy opening lines "When a man and a woman love each other very much ..." Is that actually what he said? I have no idea, and who cares. It really sucked, and I hated every second of the beginning of that conversation; although I'd relive that a thousand times to avoid what came next. He meandered through those opening sentences, explaining what we were about to talk about from a biological standpoint, without seeming invested or caring about my reaction, as if his mind was somewhere else, until his temperament shifted. Skipping over all the fundamentals that I understand are customary to such discussion, such as consent, love, respect and so on, he got right down to sex and pleasure, how good it felt; how after having sex people would feel like drug addicts on a high. He actually used that metaphor. He then went on to tell me that he was from Greece, something I knew to be completely untrue. I had met both his parents who lived in London and were English through and through. Yet still he persevered: he was indeed Greek, and in Greece it was normal for fathers to show their sons how to perform sexual acts – an assertion I was shocked by, knew to be a lie, but didn't react to. He then explained porn and masturbation to me in great detail, and how normal they were. He asked me if I had watched porn. I said no. He asked me if I wanted to. I did not give a response. He had lost interest in my physical presence by this point, and seemed more interested in weaving a story for me about how great sexual acts were. He then explained masturbation to me at great length before reverting to his previous line of storytelling, about how he was Greek and how it was normal for Greek fathers to demonstrate sexual acts to their sons. He hadn't left his spot, perched next to me on the bed, but now he stood up, lifting the blankets for me to get in.

Honestly, at this point I was in shock. Except for the words "No" and "Yes", I don't remember saying anything during this interaction which seemed to last hours, but in reality most likely lasted no more than fifteen minutes. But did it end with my being ushered into bed, as I hoped it would? No, it did not. He then slid into the bed next to me, as he had so many times before. I was tense at this point; I had not enjoyed the prior conversation and wanted it to stop, yet I had never turfed this man out of my room before, I had grown closer with him over the last year, he would talk to me for hours on the phone and text me all the time. He had parlayed with my Mum to get me a cell phone, and wasn't he supposed to be my stepfather? "Surely, this is normal", I told myself. "Surely, I can trust him." I was wrong. I felt tense and uncomfortable as he pressed his body against mine before placing a firm hand on my groin. He asked me if I had had erections before: I said "Yes". He asked me if I had one now: I said "No". He asked me if I wanted one: I didn't respond. He started to massage my groin over my trousers. I said nothing, but I wanted it to stop – I was panicking, but didn't know what to do.

When you are terrified, mentally or physically (in my case both) your body triggers the acute stress response, commonly referred to as fight or flight. Your body releases hormones to help you survive the situation, be that to fight off whatever your assailant may be or flee it entirely. A lesser known part of the acute stress response is the aspect that causes you to freeze. The fight or flight response instantaneously gears up your emergency biochemical supplies and launches them into action to protect you. You may not be so familiar with the assessment your brain makes within milliseconds of being triggered during this response. If in a fight or flight situation your brain decides that you simply cannot win, that your assailant is too powerful to be overcome, those same biochemicals, released to help you fight or escape, will, in a sense, freeze you. They act as an analgesic so that the pain inflicted upon you physically or mentally is not so unbearable. You dissociate – your body is physically present, but your faculties are essentially immobilised. Your body does this to protect you from whatever harrowing experience you are about to endure.

This is the response I experienced when Ernest decided that massaging my groin wasn't enough and decided to shove his hand down my pants and grab my penis. I would experience this response hundreds of times over the coming years. But was this the end for Ernest that evening? He hadn't finished yet – he jerked me until I was hard, a sensation that made me sick to my stomach. By this point I was out of my body, as if I was floating just above myself, looking down, watching this utterly wretched act unfold. Then he carried on stroking me, asking me if I liked what he was doing, not caring for my answer of course, his strokes getting harder and faster until I ejaculated. At that point he stopped and went quiet for a short while. He took his hands off me and sat up, telling me that I was a man now and that I should be proud. He told me that we – he used the term "we", as if I was complicit in the act, a willing volunteer – we shouldn't tell anyone about this, but that it felt good and we could do it again. At the time I just said nothing. He left the room as he came in and I lay there, waiting for my mind to return to my body. When I did wake up the next day it was like nothing had happened, yet my life was fucked from that moment on.

That was the first time he violated me, but not the last. I have tried to remember other events that took place during that week. Throughout my childhood and teenage years I can recall various family camping trips or particularly long and arduous walks in a variety of forests and put fairly accurate timeframes on them, but I can't recall much else from that week except being sexually violated by an older man. I remember wanting to escape, to run and hide; I had nowhere to go. I had left all of my friends behind when I was pulled out of Sandhurst because of a mystery slasher; I was in boarding school, so now my friends were all miles away and I didn't have their numbers. Even if I could call them, Ernest was the only one who spoke to me on that phone, and I largely associated it with him. My relationship with my Uncle Anthony had grown distant because I had shown no interest in keeping up sports, and I had been forbidden from seeing my real Dad for years now. There was no way I was talking to my Mum – we had never been particularly close – and if I wasn't comfortable divulging Ernest's evening activities to her before this, I definitely wasn't sharing what he had done now. I convinced myself that I was completely alone, trapped, as so many people do in these situations. I remember trying to escape into gaming, to avoid sleeping so I didn't have to endure another guest in my bed. That was moderately successful from what I can piece together. Perhaps the sleep deprivation is why I can recall so little else. I know that he visited me more than once that week, though on his following visits he dispensed with the niceties and just jumped straight into bed with me. When he was done with me, he was polite enough to get himself off in the bathroom, so I didn't have to see it. The bathroom was immediately adjacent to my bedroom, I could hear everything. One other detail I can recall explicitly is both my parents reprimanding me later for the phone bill I accrued during that week for internet usage. I had been spending so much time indulging in online escapism without thinking of the huge bill that dial-up connection must have been racking up. How dare I.

I returned to school after that week and intended to carry on as if nothing had changed. I locked the part of me that had been abused away in a capsule of denial and pushed it down into the depths of my mind. It wasn't all doom and gloom though, returning to school. Soon after half term my dorm mates and I were told that we would be getting moved over the Guinness house, the secondary school house. How exciting. Something had happened to me though; I couldn't quite work it out. The things I did enjoy at school I no longer wanted to partake in, and I lost interest entirely in the friend group I had. My taste in clothes and music changed drastically over the next few months, as if to reflect the disquiet raging in my subconscious. I was never an excellent student and my marks were far from exemplary, but I could apply myself when I needed to and had always enjoyed learning and would grasp topics easily. I had a general enthusiasm for life and being part of it, until it all just fell away. Like mud on a hill in the rain it washed away. My teachers likely observed this as teenage angst and the timing of the changing of houses was almost perfect for a seamless transition to a different social group entirely without anyone noticing. The phrase "dead-pan" would appear on many end-of-term report cards to describe how my teachers perceived my outlook on life.

This shift out of my boarding house into another, into a dorm full of people I didn't know, must have been like striking gold for Ernest. If I was ever going to talk to anyone about what he did to me during that half term, it would have been the small group of friends I spent my evenings with – but we had been separated now, scattered amongst the other dorms. I would never again be presented the opportunity to voice my innermost thoughts to a trusted group of friends in the black of night. Conversation before sleep in my former room had been surprisingly deep, touching on all things from thermodynamics, Maroon 5's new album and existentialism to how to get the most out of a cheap pick 'n' mix and my friend's cat, called Goose. But that friend group was dissolved, and I was presented with the challenge of making new ones – something I didn't tackle well at all. I had never been a social butterfly, or particular open with my feelings on anything, but people generally enjoyed my company as far as I could tell; I had never struggled to make new friends when moving to entirely new areas. Yet now, presented with a move to a boarding house populated by people I considered friends and some acquaintances, for some reason I gravitated towards people who I knew to be rejects and losers. Were they actually the outcasts of society? I had no idea if that's how these people were perceived by a wider audience, but that's how I saw them, and that's how I viewed myself now. After being molested I became incredibly aware that I was hiding something, afraid that at any moment someone would work out the atrocious things that had happened to me and I'd be a social pariah for ever. So I gravitated towards those people already at the bottom of the pecking order, so that I didn't have any further to fall. I began to emulate their personalities and wear them over my own like a mask to conceal my hideous secret from any prying eyes. I locked that capsule away deep down in the depths, and I planned to keep it hidden there. The feelings and memories stowed away inside would only emerge when I felt alone, or guilty. They would come on quietly at first, but as I indulged them they would begin to crash in my head like a tidal wave of incomprehensible emotion. As soon as those waves washed ashore, I would do my level best to bottle them up again and drown them once more, telling myself lies like "Ernest did nothing wrong".

The changes I have described were quite immediate, like a fuse in my brain had gone. However, they would take a while to become noticeable to anyone on the outside looking in, as I was never particularly extroverted. I abandoned my friend group and lost interest in many aspects of life. There was a further metamorphosis that occurred after my initial abuse, but it did not happen instantaneously. The Alex that existed before that half term rapidly died and was buried alongside the feelings I was denying. Over the next few months only a husk remained of my former self, and its only desire was to prevent people from learning my secret. I suspect many people observing my behaviour wrote it off as part of a teenage phase.

CHAPTER SIX

How Should *You Feel?*

I'M GOING TO take a break now from telling you my story. Frankly, I need one. What I have just written is a lot to process, and you might want some time to work through it and decide what you think. Something I was taught during my psychotherapy sessions when something affronting or upsetting was discussed was to actively sit with it. To let myself feel those emotions, really focusing on them to understand what I'm trying to feel. If you are struggling with acceptance or pain yourself – and even if you aren't, if you've decided to read this book just to expand your horizons – I would encourage you to do the same.

How did reading about a young boy being sexually abused by his slightly unstable stepfather make you feel? Think about what those feelings were: were they grief, sadness, confusion? The specific emotion isn't entirely important, just sit with it and be aware of its presence. Doing this at times when you need to process anything harrowing will prevent you from turning away from it or pushing it down. That's what I did for so long, and it did almost irreparable damage to my psyche. I wouldn't wish that on another living soul.

As an adult in my twenties, a technique I had developed in my mind, almost completely subconsciously, was to picture my abused self as a separate entity. He was me, but he was separate, a young boy standing in blackness inside my head. This version of Alex was broken and unfixable; he needed constant protection and guarding from the outside world. He had to stay hidden. He was one of those voices I would hear in the cacophony I mentioned in the first chapter – his voice would be added and would scream to be released no matter how.

How on earth does someone who is broken begin fixing themselves? I'm not a professional, and I frankly just don't know. I did pick up some helpful information during my journey of recovery, and I'll share it with you now. Ready?

First, you don't do it alone. Perhaps there are people out there who can achieve that, but I certainly wasn't one of them. I was only damaging myself by trying, and I wouldn't recommend it for you either. Second, you are not broken; there will be damage, but it can be repaired with the right tools. You may feel broken, or you may perceive another survivor of abuse in this manner, but you/they are not. If you do insist on using "broken" as a metaphor, at least finish the sentence "but not beyond repair". The only ones broken in this scenario are the abusers who inflict their torment knowingly without remorse.

I have touched on my encounters with therapy in this book so far, and I will again. I make no apologies for that; without therapy I wouldn't be here. I owe many people the life I have today – most of all my wife, Thea – but I certainly wouldn't be where I am today without the efforts of my therapists. You may be surprised just how therapeutic therapy can be, whatever the medium you choose. Some counsellors hold group sessions, others have one-on-one sessions, some try to work outdoor activity into their sessions, and some offer a mix of everything. I hope you seek out counselling and therapy, and I hope you keep trying to find what works for you until something does. There are so many great people and services out there, and they may not all work for you, but something will. Someone can help you. I visited several different therapists and services throughout the process of bringing what happened to me to light and sometimes just turning up to those appointments was a struggle, but they were worth it in the end. I'm beginning to sound like a cracked record, so I'll stop if you promise me one thing: *don't do this alone.*

And again, *you are not broken.* You may be all bent out of shape, but that kind of damage can be repaired. Your abuser might have broken your bones and shattered your psyche, performed other untold horrors upon you, but with time and help you can heal. You can come back from anything. The human being is famously tenacious and resilient. You may have told yourself that you are broken, you may have been told by others that you are broken beyond repair, but it is just not true.

You might remember earlier in the book I mentioned the acute stress response. I'm no professional, but I have sat in rooms with professionals for long periods of time, time which I paid for out of my own pocket, and so I feel comfortable sharing some of the things I learnt during these sessions with you. Specifically, biochemical responses.

As we discussed earlier, when you are terrified by an assailant your acute stress response is triggered – the key words here being acute: *"of severe and short duration"*. That's only the initial response to abuse, though. We know that the stress doesn't subside after the triggering event; the panic should, but the accompanying stress, worry, fear and wretchedness are here to stay until you can be rid of them. So what does that do to you? Ongoing or chronic stress will cause you severe damage.

Not all stress is bad, mind you; there are people out there whose fight-or-flight response has saved them from a terrible fate, and others who managed to get that big project at work turned in on time because they got stressed out and worked harder than ever before. But in such situations these people are then able to shut off their varying stress responses, we assume for the sake of this discussion anyway, and return to their normal states of being.

Chronic stress will lead to elevated levels of cortisol being pumped through your system, cortisol being the stress hormone. It will also result in reduced serotonin, dopamine and some other neurotransmitters. These chemicals all combine in a normal, happy, healthy and otherwise well-functioning human being to control things we do every day: our sleep, our moods, sex drive, our appetites and even our energy levels.

If your stress response doesn't power down after an event, maybe because your tormenter is still in the house living with you and could strike again at any moment, the ongoing stress can very easily lead to severe depression. Hell, let's be honest, even being on the periphery of an event such as sexual abuse towards a child is enough to inflict depression on just about anyone, I think.

But back to the case in point. Now I am going to start using the term *when* rather than *if*, because I think if you have been subjected to a traumatic event such as sexual abuse and don't receive the proper help, it truly is a matter of when. When depression visits you, like it did me, you will likely begin to experience changes that you might not have expected or intended. Often depressed people, unintentionally and through no fault of their own, neglect basic self-care and healthy lifestyle choices (I am using that last term to encompass everything from social wellbeing to physical exercise and everything in between), which in turn can lead to deeper, darker chronic stress and depression, and ultimately a self-perpetuating cycle of harm. An Ouroboros of pain, if you will. But all that damage comes from an identifiable source, it is reparable. You are not broken.

An interesting anecdote I picked up whilst perusing a medical journal published in 2010 is that those of us who have battled or are battling with depression are far more likely to experience the freeze reaction of fight-or-flight. This particular study showed that people battling depression actually exhibited strong feelings of anger, or *fight*, and an overwhelming desire to run, or *flight*, but could do neither and instead froze – or, as this journal described it, *"bec[a]me blocked, inhibited, and arrested, which increased stress"*. What a cruel system.

I have shared these brief thoughts and short explanations I received from other much smarter people simply to highlight that you are not broken, I was not broken. The feelings I and you have experienced are the result of a bio-chemical reaction triggered by our brains with the best of intention, to protect us. This, cruelly, resulted in our abusers inflicting even more damage to us via a chemical imbalance in our brain, resulting in chronic stress and depression. I don't mean to diagnose you, but there's a very good chance you can recognise the symptoms and if you honestly reflect on it, you'll know if you exhibit them or not. That chemical imbalance is what makes you feel so wretched, it's what makes you feel trapped and unworthy like you're swimming in a giant black void, hopelessly paddling through the cesspit of life with no purpose other than to survive until your next encounter with your abuser. Those chemical reactions, those awful occurrences taking place in your brain have been studied to the moon and back by medical professionals, and here's the good news: as a result of all that research they can help you fix them. It's not my place to tell you to seek medical help, but it wasn't my place to tell you to seek counselling or therapy either. I didn't make you pick up this book or read this far, I have simply recounted my tale and thrown some advice in with it – advice which I took myself. As a result I am here today, happy and healthy, and ready to help as many people as I possibly can. If I were you, I'd find someone to help you with the mental aspect of your abuse, and someone to help you with the chemical aspects of your abuse. Let's talk about the emotional aspect first.

Do you want to know what I think the most important part of any emotional response is? (Bearing in mind this is coming from someone who will admit they didn't properly feel their emotions until they were in their twenties.) I think the most important part of emotions is just feeling them. Whatever it is, whatever you've got, just feel it and let it be with you. Don't chase it away. I said that at the top of this chapter, and I am saying it again because it's important. If you want me to tell you how to feel you are going to be disappointed, because I won't do that. But what I will say is that if you have suffered abuse and you've gotten to the point where you can feel again, or if you managed to never let go of those emotions, then I applaud your tenacity. You are already braver than I ever was. I can't imagine surviving whilst holding onto those emotions, it would have been hell. My brain shut off the emotional processing functions of the amygdala and diverted power elsewhere.

Would you like to know what I felt when I finally came to terms with my emotions again and was able to process what I was feeling? After hours of paid psychotherapy sessions and counselling? After keeping a secret from the person I love the most in the world for years? Hate. Pure, seething hatred. When I realised what it was, I almost had to shut it off again for fear of what I would do with it; I wanted to hurt him. I wanted to punish him for all the things he did to me; I felt as if violence would be justified. Those thoughts weren't safe, and they were the result of uncorking a bottle full of built-up pressure after years of repression. I was lucky enough to pull that cork in an environment where I was safe and supported, with access to information to help me work through my feelings. If I had done that under different circumstances, I'm not sure where I would have ended up – I may still be writing this book, but likely under quite different circumstances.

Hate is what I felt; hatred for him, everything he put me through, and the pain he caused my family, the pain I would need to expose them to by revealing who he really was. You are likely processing what you have just read and thinking, "Hate, hmm? That doesn't sound healthy or very in tune with the zeitgeist." You may even wish to oppose me, or tell me that I shouldn't feel hate – that it isn't proper, or correct. Some people have tried to tell me I should forgive him. I have no argument to support why hate is any better than the multitude of other emotions you may feel or courses of action you may choose to take; hate is what I felt. My recovery from his vile torment was drenched in hatred for him, and I will make no apologies for it. It is my belief that what you feel isn't the most important aspect, it's allowing yourself to feel and deciding a course of action to take, bringing those feelings along with you.

Sitting in therapy at the time I had my emotional epiphany, I already knew that I wanted to mend the damage done to me and seek justice for his crimes against me; and now I had fuel. Initially, I was primed to go and pull the filthy vermin's head off his shoulders. Fortunately, I was in the appropriate place with a professional to guide me through those raw emotions, help me achieve clarity, and target my rage appropriately. This is important because, for one thing, pulling anyone's head off – even a paedophile rapist's head – would be considered murder. And murder is bad. Secondly, simply getting pissed off and running around wild whilst trying to achieve a constructive and healing outcome for myself and my family just simply wouldn't work. It isn't *what* you feel that is important, it's the *act* of allowing yourself to feel your emotions and then choose how to use them. Therapy facilitated that for me, and it can work for you.

Perhaps you will feel despondency and self-loathing. Those feelings are not invalid, but they are likely muddled messages from your biochemically imbalanced brain, because you are worth saving, you can be helped, and things *will* get better. Therapy, counselling and even medical help, if you are open to them, can help you work through the feelings and focus them in a constructive way. They can work for you in the same way they did for me and can assist you should you seek closure and justice. I am living proof of that.

I'd like to quickly revisit my epiphany before I give anyone a false sense of the efficacy of therapy. I had this epiphany, it is true, but whilst the realisation dawned on me rapidly, it had a long prior incubation period. All the events that came beforehand were precursors to that realisation. Isaac Newton may have first thought of gravity upon seeing an apple fall from a tree, yet he would likely have carried on regardless had he not experienced and been exposed to everything else in his life prior to that pivotal moment.

If you don't want to take any of my advice, that's fine. If you think I'm full of shit, that's ok too. But from one compassionate human being to another, do something for me, ok? Just talk to someone. A friend, a loved one, a professional, or an anonymous support line – just find a friendly ear and talk to them, please.

CHAPTER SEVEN

Spain

RIGHT – I'M FEELING a little bit better for that short break away, after recounting my first encounter with my abuser once he had revealed himself in his true form. Are you? I hope so, because I regret to inform you that we aren't even close to being done. I will assume that by this point you the reader don't need a blow by blow account of my daily school life, or for me to go into explicit detail of each night that creep climbed into my bed, so I'm going to start moving through the years at a slightly greater pace. While retelling my story as accurately as I can is important to me, I don't want to bore you with too many details. With that in mind, let's get on with it.

I am in the ninth year of my schooling now, fourteen years old going on fifteen, and life is beyond miserable. I can confidently state that there has been a steady decline in my academic performance, attendance of just about everything, and general attitude. During term time I spend my nights staring into nothing, and parts of my days in class sleeping. By this point I have taken up smoking whenever cigarettes are available, which is essentially all the time, and drinking any alcohol I can get my hands on.

At home, Ernest's promotion produced more money around the house. We were able to go away as a family on holiday more than once a year now if we wanted. But because that money didn't immediately settle the various household debts, the next family holiday was a camping one. Ernest had managed to purchase himself a new camera with the bump in salary, though it was never produced around the family. This camera, which I never actually saw myself, was only brought out at night when he was done with me. Once he was satisfied and had enough, he would pull my pants down, if they weren't already, and put me in some compromising position – all whilst I did my best to feign sleep – then take pictures. I knew he was taking pictures because I would hear the lens extending when the camera was turned on, hear the beep as it focused, and my peripheral vision would light up with the flash. They say once it's on the internet it's there forever, and I have no doubt that is where the pictures ended up.

So, we're going camping. Some teens would baulk at the concept of camping, and I suspect I probably did too. After giving it some thought, though, I realised that ten days with the whole family in a small tent in a field over half term meant I would be able to spend my half term free of any nighttime visits and without any worry about being caught on camera. I remember feeling an overwhelming sense of relaxation and relief over this half term: I fell asleep in the sun, laughed with my brothers, and even got to know some of the other kids my age at the campsite. It's incredible how much of a mental shift occurs when the looming threat of sexual abuse is lifted from your shoulders.

One afternoon at the campsite, a girl younger than me by what I thought was a couple of years approached the tent whilst I was lounging in the sun and asked if I had a phone. Cautiously, I said yes. Any mention of my phone brought about a deepseated feeling of unease that would cause my stomach to knot uncomfortably ... Ernest was the only person who communicated with me via phone. But for the most part I don't think any of that came across as the girl asked for my number, saying that her older sister had asked for it. She even told me I should come to their tent later in the evening, and pointed it out to me.

That evening was like being in a dream world. I was hanging out with other kids my age, and one of them was a girl who was interested in me, it seemed. We hung out as a group under the stars, talking and playing games; in those moments I didn't give a second's thought to Ernest or what awaited me the next time I returned home. I was free, I was being a teenager. Like I had hit the jackpot at the end of the evening when it was time to turn in, the girl who had asked for my number (who we will refer to as Clare) wanted to know if I was single. Of course I made my availability known – how could I not? I was carefree in those moments, not a worry in the world. We would continue our relationship via text from then on, but I didn't see her again for a while.

Once the holiday was over I returned to school. The sense of freedom I had felt whilst camping left me as soon as we started packing down the tent. By now I had given up on academia, there was no hope for me, and it didn't matter what anyone did or said, I was simply not interested. Homework? That might get done, but only if I could do it in the ten minutes at the start of a class prior to the teacher remembering having set some. Any kind of collaborative project? Sorry. I genuinely feel sorry for those kids lumped with me who wanted to do well and achieve. I did not give a fuck. My uniform was filthy, my body unwashed, and my attitude matched.

By this point most of my clothes had been replaced with something black and baggy, paired with a choice in music chosen specifically to offend and drive people away. But I had something keeping me going here, I had someone interested in me who was willing to talk to me on a daily basis despite knowing next to nothing about me. Through the joy of the SMS I could portray myself as anyone. As far as Clare knew I was a windswept, interesting, underachieving genius who was really doing the school a favour by gracing them with my presence. I would regularly have to clear time out of my busy social schedule just to text her. Because Clare had no way of ever finding out about the denial I had hidden away, I could be anyone with her; I had nothing to hide. There was a strange dichotomy at play: physically and mentally I was completely checked out and believed myself to be worthless, yet I still had this desire to be loved and succeed. A sad teenage torment, perhaps a cliché.

But I promised you we were going to pick up the pace. By now I had started doing anything I could to avoid going home because I knew what was waiting for me there. There were occasions where some well-to-do individual would confront me about avoiding home, maybe a teacher, sometimes my Mum or a friend. When faced with these situations I would return home and accept my fate at the hands of Ernest. It was easier to deny anything was wrong so I wouldn't have to face prying eyes. Easier to accept the inevitable, humiliating abuse than face further questioning as to why I was trying to avoid home.

For the most part I was successful in my endeavours to avoid home – and Ernest by extension – but there were times when this simply wasn't an option, one example being school holidays. The next one was coming around really quickly, and it was going to be a real "treat" for us all. Having achieved a little more financial padding with Ernest's new salary, this time around our family would be going to Spain. This should have been a happy thing for me; I should have shared in the excitement with my brothers, I should have emulated the happiness in my mother's voice when she announced where we were going. Instead I protested in a juvenile manner, told my Mum I hated the idea, and would rather stay home or at school while they holidayed without me. This caused more arguments and tension, further degrading the relationship between the two of us. But as was inevitable, we all ended up in Spain.

The theme park Port Aventura was the goal of our visit – quite a lively place absolutely overrun with British tourists. We were packed into that park like tuna in a net. Cigarette smoke hung over the crowds waiting for rides like a dense smog, the smell of cheap booze and body odour caressing the nostrils. The rides themselves were enormous, their gargantuan frames towering over us like behemoths. It was a foul place, but it was the first time my brothers had ever witnessed a proper theme park, and my Mum was excited to have been able to bring them there.

Our stay was not in Port Aventura itself but at a nearby hotel complex, the kind that supplies its guests with small apartment-style accommodation, a central communal swimming pool and all-you-can-eat buffet dinners. Think Benidorm. As a family, we needed two separate apartments to house us for our stay. This was a complete lie, a single room would have happily housed all of us, especially as we were accustomed to sharing a tent. But no, two rooms is what we got. One for my brothers and Mum; one for myself and Ernest. With the security of a locked door behind us, in the privacy of his own space he escalated the abuse. This short trip away was the first time he penetrated me. It hurt me a great deal – he didn't use lubrication. This would occur each and every night we were there. By the third night I was begging my Mum for coins when we returned from the theme park for the day. I wanted to buy as much online time at the hotel internet café as I could, to escape into some online games and pretend I was someone else whilst chatting with Clare on MSN. This triggered a very negative response from my Mum, and then me in turn; how ungrateful of me, she must have thought. Given the evidence she was presented with that was fair enough – the family had forked out so much extra cash for a holiday overseas, and all her eldest son wanted to do was play on the internet and talk to his girlfriend! How selfish.

Eventually she caved, and I dashed away to avoid Ernest for as long as I could. I was there for what seemed like hours, long after Clare had logged off and the internet had proved too slow to play anything. I spoke to the other kids around the computers until they all left. I thought surely

Ernest would have fallen asleep by now, surely he wouldn't be waiting for me if I went back to the room ... and then he appeared beside me. He wanted to know how much longer I would be, if I was done with the computer, and if I would like a drink. Out of the options presented to me I opted for the drink. We sat at this bar adjacent to the computers talking to the bartender (who spoke great English) about our day as if we were a normal father and son, tired from a day's excitement and about to get some rest before doing it all again. Once that drink was finished we walked back to the room. He walked a few steps behind me talking the whole way; it was as if I was being escorted, frogmarched back to my cell. This night, as 'punishment' for what I assume he considered my trying to avoid him (and he would have been right), he had me perform oral sex on him. There was only a double bed in the room as it had been booked for two people, so we had to share it; I had no other option except the cold tile floor. He got into that bed as soon as we got back to the room and I went into the bathroom to clean my teeth. I stayed in there for as long as possible, trying to delay the inevitable advances and painful penetration. I didn't expect that once I entered the room again I would have to perform oral sex on my stepfather. But that is how it happened. He made his sick demand in the form of a request, but when I obliged, it became clear that I was incapable of satisfying him; he withdrew from my mouth and wanted my arse. I was sickened and distraught whilst he had his way with me. While I had been abused frequently, until now I had just been able to shut down and mentally go somewhere else; drift off and dissociate from reality in the safe place in my mind, where I could deny everything that was happening. But now I had to perform a deplorable act for my survival and discard whatever shred of dignity I had left. I felt utter humiliation. He finished and I cleaned myself off in the usual fashion before having to get back into bed with him. I was not going to sleep that night. Or much any night after, for a long while.

The holiday continued in that fashion. I was there for his entertainment and pleasure in the evenings and presented for family photos during the day. I'd entertain myself whilst on the rides thinking about the safety barriers failing while the rides were upside down, so that I could plunge to my death during what I perceived would be a happy coincidence. The ride would end, we'd queue up for the next one as a family, he would get into the ride beside me, and I'd do the same thing again until it was over. I don't remember the second half of that holiday, and my memories of the immediate months after are also severely fragmented – so I can't articulate to you the end of that trip or much of the weeks to come. The expression I tried to display outwardly, captured in my report card, was "dead pan", but inside I was utterly distraught and disgusted with myself; I felt wretched to my core. I was fourteen years old and I wanted to die.

With each new abuse Ernest inflicted upon me I found another part of myself fracturing. Pieces of who I was were falling away, relegated to the ever-expanding oceans of my mind reserved for denial. Soon an involuntary internal dialogue would wash up with the memories and emotions I was trying to deny, apologising for Ernest's actions; it would assure me that he was unwell, that he did it because he cared, or – by far the worst lie – that I *wanted* him to do those things to me.

My memories of returning to the UK from that trip are a hazy blur for the most part. With effort on my behalf, support from my wife, and guidance from counsellors, I have been able to piece together the fragments of my memory into an almost complete timeline to create this book. But for some time after that trip all I can recall is distressed distortion. I remember fighting with Clare over the phone because I stopped talking to her online whilst in Spain and didn't text her when I got back to the UK. Not the type of thing a confident, compassionate and intelligent underachieving guy would do – of course that wasn't who I was, but how was she to know?

But I can remember why I didn't text her when I got back home. The reason is beyond fucked up: I felt like I had been unfaithful. Up until that third night I had only been raped. But on that third night I convinced myself that I had willingly performed fellatio on him. I hated myself, everything I was; this notion was supported by the sinister dialogue in my head. Everything he had done to me was *him, he* performed those actions and made those decisions; but I convinced myself that *I* chose to perform oral sex and by doing so justified every foul thing he had done to me. Clare and I broke up; my lifeline, my escape from reality where I could portray myself as anyone, was gone.

The rest of my school year is lost to me. I know nothing more than that it happened. There are some less than flattering school reports, but I couldn't tell you much else about that time – except that at the end of that school year something incomprehensible occurred. Another girl was interested in me, or so one of my fellow boarder friends told me. Apparently teenage girls had a thing for gaunt, deadbeat, no-prospect losers. Weird. What I was told was true, and whilst confusing, this girl's interest in me may have prevented me from walking myself into the path of oncoming traffic. The prospect that someone out there could like me made me feel wanted.

I acknowledge that this was a very self-serving way of seeing things. I lacked any kind of confidence or ability to talk to her face to face, so I did what I did best. I had the friend get her number for me, and we began to text. We interacted in person from time to time – this was unavoidable when you attend and live in the same school – but I was able to maintain a ruse for the time we were in each other's company. Sarah was clearly interested in deadbeats and I knew how to play that role well – I just had to hide the crippling neuroses, insecurities and depression that were settling in. Summer holidays were fast approaching, and I would need to return home, back into his clutches. However, by this point I had convinced Sarah of the alternate personality I had shown her, and we were in a relationship. I would spend the summer projecting a false personality into Sarah's mind and escape into that story. I would survive these holidays by using Sarah in the same way I used Clare: as a distraction from being raped.

CHAPTER EIGHT

Mind Games and Manipulation

AT THIS POINT in my life I had not breathed a word of what was happening to me to another soul. The majority of my waking hours I spent actively denying that any cruel fate had befallen me, an effort which took up much of my cognitive bandwidth. There were times when all of the feelings I was denying and shoving down would bubble up, and looking back, I definitely had opportunities to share them. My Uncle Anthony and aunt would visit, I could have spoken to them; any member of my family likely would have listened. I should have told my Mum, but I felt I couldn't. There was a phone in my hand or pocket at almost every hour of the day now, I could have called the police and been saved (maybe); but I refrained. I chose not to say a word because I was in denial, frightened and damaged to the point of beginning to apologise for his actions. This man had power over me.

Just the thought of speaking about what was happening to me to another person gave me a headache. And even then, if I spoke to someone, why would they believe me? I was a deadbeat, bad-attitude loser who made no effort to do well in life; he was an Army officer, he had served overseas, went to church and paid taxes. If I spoke, who would save me from him? I knew he was stronger and faster than me; I could wait to tell someone at school, but I convinced myself that no teacher would believe me, that none of them wanted anything to do with me. Besides, if he found out I told someone at school I was certain he would release those pictures he had taken of me, if he hadn't already, and at the time that seemed a worse fate. And my Mum: even though our relationship was severely damaged by my behaviour, I still loved her. She would be destroyed if she found out what was happening. There was no conceivable choice for me other than to keep my mouth shut; I felt as if I had been buried alive, completely trapped.

I would think through scenarios of crying out for help for the whole drive home with Ernest, who always picked me up from school for holidays. This particular summer holiday was going to be a bad one. He talked to me the whole way home like there was nothing going on between us, like he hadn't been sexually abusing me for his own amusement, raping me, taking pictures of me naked from the waist down. He'd talk to me like he was my stepfather and I was his son, then he would rest his hand on my inner thigh just below my crotch, as if to remind me that I was his.

Online games were my solace this summer. I would go without sleep and spend every waking hour I could "wasting my youth". The computer was tucked away in the now-familiar study room, with its street-facing window from which the roof of the garage could be accessed. When I was able, during the night if no one else was awake, I would climb out and smoke whatever cigarettes I had out there. The more time I spent in the study trying to combat Ernest's ability to loom over me, the more time he would find to spend in there with me. I don't know how he managed to do it, as he had two other children he was meant to be looking after and a household to maintain. Obviously, monitoring my activities and looking for an opportune moment to get what he wanted from me was more important.

Time passed slowly during that period, at least as I remember it. Ernest soon started telling me that he loved me and that he believed we should be in a relationship. He told me that he loved my Mum and my brothers, but he wanted to be with me. In some twisted manner I let myself believe parts of what he was saying. I was tired of the denial, and it was easier to accept some of the poison he dripped in my ear than try and argue. I couldn't accept that we were in a relationship or that he loved me – he wouldn't do the things he did to me if that were true, I knew that. But I accepted that he believed those things he was telling me; it was easier that way. Accepting reality would be to live every day knowing that he was simply an evil, possibly sick, twisted man who would rape me whenever he saw fit and photograph the aftermath for his viewing pleasure when I wasn't around. Living a delusion was simpler. Just as it was simpler to keep my mouth shut, accept my fate and avoid conversation with anyone who would express concern for me.

I know he said those things in an attempt to stop me shutting down when he wanted to rape me, to turn me into a willing participant. He thought if he told me he loved me then I would love him back. His words had the opposite effect; I didn't think I could drift any deeper into my mind, but somehow I did. I would forgo eating, drinking, sleeping and washing whilst home, and escape further into my games, just try and be somewhere else. Just escape. I would wake up from crashing in my chair after countless hours gaming and not know where I was or even *who* I was at times. I became entirely addicted to the escapism offered to me through on-line games. My Mum might wake me up some mornings and I wouldn't be able to converse with her in a coherent manner at all. When I came to, I would lash out at her and drive her out of the room aggressively. I didn't want to be reminded of my life, I wanted to escape it.

The only thing I chose to do outside of my gaming world was to communicate with Sarah, trying to maintain that relationship so that I had a story to escape into when I returned to school. I attempted to sculpt an image of myself in her mind as a nonchalant, aloof character with more to offer than I really did. Lying to her about my existence was quite fun and made me feel good. This was an unfair manipulation, and I am sorry for that now. I think I may have lost all ties to reality – a term I use loosely, as our interactions weren't exactly genuine, obsessed as I was with building a character profile to assume once I returned to school.

There was no escape from Ernest by text with Sarah, though; she wouldn't always text back fast enough for me to ignore him. The only thing I could throw myself into enough to transcend the situation was gaming. I had even found one online game which had a voice chat function, so I could tell him my microphone was on. He would leave me be for a time until he got frustrated and simply unplugged the microphone.

Eventually he lost his patience with me dodging his advances. One night he came into the room, demanded I stand up, pulled down my pants, then and proceeded to jerk himself hard. He then sat in the chair himself. My game was still going, and I just stood there looking at the monitor and then him, the only light in the room coming from the monitor, illuminating his face which was bent in a grin. He told me to carry on playing, so I did, and he just sat there behind me until he quietly told me to sit down. I didn't obey and he said it again, followed by putting his hand on my hips and pulling me down on top of him. It hurt, as it had hurt every time before, as he raped me. When he was finished with me I had to go and clean myself off in the bathroom. I locked the door behind me and cried. I was no longer safe in my world of gaming.

A state of crisis was declared in my mind. Up until this time I had been able to avoid him by ignoring his presence and when that was no longer an option I could disconnect from the world, submit myself to him and allow whatever was going to happen, happen. But now all I had was submission. I could no longer seek reprieve in my pixelated world. Soon I found myself obsessing over the notion that this man actually loved me. If he loved me, was it fair for me to ignore him in this way? Perhaps all this time I was spending gaming to avoid him was unfair. I genuinely found myself having thoughts like that. Physically resisting him had never been an option for me, but I had always kept a strong barrier between my world and his in my mind. Now even that was starting to wane. He was beginning to get inside my head and make me rethink what I thought I knew. For the longest time a part of me knew that Ernest had molested me, but I was in denial. I was too ashamed to tell anyone, and too afraid of the consequences that would be felt by my family if I were to reveal who this man truly was. But now I started questioning myself: I was keeping his filthy secret, but perhaps it was my secret too. This man was telling me he loved me, and outside of his sexual acts he was not outwardly cruel to me – he housed, clothed and fed me. Isn't that love?

When Ernest first told me he loved me and wanted a relationship with me, I accepted that he believed his words, but also thought he was mentally unwell, which rendered those thoughts meaningless. But now I became concerned about the morality of what I was doing: was I the one taking advantage of him by not saying anything to anyone? Was I the abuser? Reflecting now upon this mindset shift makes me feel sick. It's clear to me now that I was starting to feel the effects of Stockholm Syndrome: I was beginning to develop sympathy for him after being trapped in this situation for so long. The weight of the abuse and my living situation was proving to be too much. My last sanctum, the escapism offered through gaming, had been breached. There was little I could do to avoid reality now.

In his book *Man's Search for Meaning*, Viktor E Frankl wrote: "*When a man finds that it is his destiny to suffer, he will have to accept his suffering as his task; his single and unique task. He will have to acknowledge the fact that even in suffering his is unique and alone in the universe. No one can relieve him of his suffering or suffer in his place. His unique opportunity lies in the way in which he bears his burden.*" I do not have the audacity to compare myself to Frankl, or what he or his people endured. To do that I would have to be out of my mind. But I did suffer, and I bore my suffering in my own unique way for many years. In a way, writing this account is yet another way in which I do so.

The last of my summer holidays passed. Ernest did not get what I believe he hoped for from me, which was a more active sexual partner. But once I started to allow myself to believe he loved me, interacting with him as just a guy I lived with became easier, and he responded in kind. He started buying me things, like clothes and gadgets. I even went back to school with a new MP3 player. Obviously, he was pleased with his progress with me.

Returning to school for my tenth year with this new baggage weighing on my mind was harder than usual. Normally I would simply hate myself and feel quite depressed; now I started to feel deep, strong pangs of guilt – guilt for the wrongdoing I was convincing myself I was inflicting upon my stepfather. I worried that I was the catalyst behind whatever had caused him to begin molesting me, and deserving of the abuse I received because of this. He was clearly unwell, and I knew you should never offer an alcoholic drink was this the same thing? By simply being a kid around a paedophile had I committed some atrocious act? Having the music to listen to at night made it easier to sleep. I simply tried to forget that he had bought me the MP3 player.

Now that I was fifteen years old, any chance of my moods being recognised as 'off' had completely gone. Just about every kid in the boarding house was off sulking or acting out in some way or another. I was just another teenager like everyone else, part of the veritable orchestra of hormones ringing out in an angsty pubescent disharmony. My moods were not the result of a phase, though. They were justified; each time I would leave home and return to school I brought with me a whole new complex to contend with. Almost every time I saw Ernest he would add another dimension to the abuse.

Fortunately, I now had a task with which to distract myself. I had spent a lot of time over the summer escaping into a made-up world that I was creating for Sarah; I wanted her to know as little truth about me as possible, so that she would want to continue her relationship with me. I had crafted my personal character profile, and now that I was back at school I would need to get into character. I didn't feel good about this manipulation at the time; I felt bad for lying about who I was, but I was desperate to create an escape from reality, and playing a made-up character was as close as I could get. For the most part my faux romantic endeavours with her were successful, meaning I think she felt too bad for me to end the relationship. Perhaps she was worried how she would be perceived, ending things so quickly, I don't know. I had mastered the art of pretending to be asleep and even taking my consciousness off to some faraway place in my mind, but acting like someone a girl would actually be interested in was beyond me. I was too desperate to feel wanted, which led to incredibly needy behaviour on my behalf. I was undeniably a deadbeat, though, and I think she liked that. My neurotic behaviour was outweighed by that – for now at least.

Sarah and I continued to see each other through the term, and it soon became clear to me not only that she was useful for the occasional dopamine rush that would come each time she actually wanted to spend time with me, but that I could also shield myself from Ernest by brandishing the relationship between Sarah and me in front of him. On the occasions where I had to return home, he would ritualistically come to my room towards the end of the evening when he expected to be able to take advantage of me. At this time, I still believed that in his own sick way he loved me. Whilst this was a clear downturn in my mental state, it did enable me to talk to him when he appeared in my room. When I solely saw him as my tormenter, as a terrifying force existing only to inflict suffering on me, I was too scared to say anything that might upset him; but with the notion that he loved me floating around in my brain, I still felt disgusted by myself, but less threatened by his presence. I would tell him that things between Sarah and I were getting serious, and that I didn't want him getting into bed with me because I would feel unfaithful towards her. For some reason this worked. I think that drawing a comparison between the relationship I had established with Sarah and him visiting me at night gave him satisfaction. But the protection that flaunting Sarah gave me did not last forever; the more I used it, the less effective it became. When Sarah did save me from having to satisfy him, I would use the time to climb out the window onto the garage, smoke cigarettes and text her.

Quite unhealthily, I started to see her as a saviour figure, my protector. I put her on a pedestal in my mind. Having an emotionally detached, rather unhygienic, deadbeat yet incredibly clingy and needy guy hanging around you and texting you all the time must have been awful for her. She grew more distant from me each day as the school year went on. I can't blame her for that, but it did prompt me to make a decision. She was my reluctant guardian angel; she had, inadvertently, protected me from Ernest's advances more than anyone else in my life. I decided that she needed to know why I behaved the way I did, why I was who I was. I made a decision to tell her everything. I was going to let go of the denial and tell someone what Ernest was doing to me. The outcome of that decision not only ended our relationship, but prompted me to decide to forget everything that ever happened to me: to suppress and move on.

In a fashion typical of myself at the time, I was formulating indirect methods of sharing my secret with Sarah. Talking to her – or anyone – face to face really wasn't my forte. My modus operandi at the time was to text, but the keypad layout on my cell phone (and all cell phones at the time) made pouring my heart and soul out rather a challenge. The task was made easier with the application of text abbreviations, but that hardly seemed appropriate. I toyed with the idea of writing her a letter – I could lay out everything I wanted her to know on paper, and give it to her as we parted ways on any given evening. Give her an insight into the innermost depths of my life and mind through the medium of the written word. I actually started writing that letter before screwing it up and starting over, again and again.

There was also the challenge of using any form of eloquent language. I wanted to weave a story for Sarah like a metaphorical tapestry, but any particular command of the English language I may have possessed at the time deserted me. I mentioned earlier in the book that emotions, like muscles, need to be exercised in order to best function; the same applies to language. I may not have been loquacious, but I desired to be able to communicate beyond my basic vernacular in this letter. Unfortunately I had been less than attentive in my pursuit of academic prowess, and found myself unable. That's a longwinded way of saying that there was no way in hell I was going to make myself look even more stupid by writing to her by hand. I also had terrible handwriting, so there's that too.

I was haunted for days by the thought of telling Sarah how I had been treated at home. I wanted to tell her that she had saved me from being raped on many occasions, and that I was eternally grateful. I just didn't know how to effectively communicate. Perhaps, I thought, I wouldn't tell her anything; maybe that would be better.

Whilst I am under no illusion about the way a teenage girl would react to that news, especially from me, I wish I had written that letter. She may have given it to her tutors, probably after showing all her friends first, but then someone may have gotten me help. Unfortunately, that missive never came to be. One of the weekends where I had no choice but to return home, following another emotionally and physically destructive evening, not before much internal strife, I caved to my desire to tell Sarah and started drafting a text. Keep in mind that this was on a three-letter-per-number contemporary phone keyboard. It was going to take a long time for me to weave this tapestry. The first draft never got sent, it just sat on my phone; but I did get up the courage to send her a message implying that my stepfather had been violent towards me on occasions. Sarah immediately responded to this text, which I did not expect. She expressed genuine concern and worry; I definitely didn't expect that. And she went on to say she was going to help me – this was too much. I was overwhelmed at the concept of all of this coming out, and I hadn't even told the whole truth. I panicked, and desperately tried to walk back my story. I said it had only ever happened once, it wasn't that bad – I was sure he didn't mean it, and there was no need for her to worry. After some back and forth in that fashion she accepted my explanation and let the matter go. I had lied and then lied again, lessened Ernest's crimes towards me and then defended him to the person I intended to spill my guts to. I felt pathetic.

Mentally exhausted, I decided to leave my room in which this back and forth had occurred, leaving my phone on the windowsill. A tension headache had rapidly set in during the text exchange and I just needed to step away. Leaving my phone anywhere was not a habit I was in since I had first been given a phone, briefed as I was that at any time someone could be monitoring my conversations, and told to watch for his symbol. After experiencing such concern about the privacy of my phone communications, I was shocked upon returning to my room to find it in Ernest's hands.

I had a red Motorola Razor, quite a new phone at the time. It had a fancy metallic keyboard and it would snap when I closed it. That was such a satisfying sound; I would hold that phone in my hand, open the screen slightly and let it snap back just to hear the sound. But there was no satisfaction from it this time as I entered, sounding louder than ever as he forced it quickly shut, shoving it back onto the windowsill where it had been. I don't know why he bothered – I hadn't reported him for any of his crimes yet, so I was hardly going to dob him in for snooping through my phone. Perhaps he was worried about damaging whatever relationship he thought he was building with me; perhaps he aspired to build a trusting rapport with me. Over the years many of the fumes he would spew around me seeped into my thoughts, causing me to believe and feel certain things, but I was still confident I would never trust him. But why would he snoop around like this? He could have just demanded the phone from me – he was paying for it, after all. Maybe he was just embarrassed about being caught in the act.

One thing did become clear very quickly: he had read my messages to Sarah, at least the ones that had been sent – and I would later find the draft I wrote deleted. Between shoving the phone down and walking over to me he mumbled something like, "You have to be careful what you say in case your Mum reads these", as if the texts I was sending were the most worrying thing she could find out. As he approached me, he drew himself up to his full height. I am fairly sure that by this point in my life I was taller than him, but I felt small and insignificant. He tried to look me in the eyes, but I avoided his gaze. He began with an angry tone, almost barking: "Think about what you're doing. You can tell people about us if you want. But think about what would happen to your mother, think about what it would do to her." Then his tone softened, as if he was hurt or sad: "Think about your brothers' lives. They would have to grow up without a father." And with even more pain in his voice, trying once more to catch my gaze, "I would go to prison, you would be taking me away from the boys."

His intended manipulation was completely successful. My entire perspective shifted from this point forward for years to come, his words echoing in my head. I felt he was pleading with me, for lack of a better term, and his words continued to reverberate. He used the term "us", he loved me, and I believed that. I had hurt this sick man who was only expressing his love for me, the man who had housed and fed me for all this time. And my family – how selfish of me, unfairly trying to tell outside parties our business! Had I no shame? I would have caused them such great pain. I should be grateful for what I had, I should just deal with the hand fate dealt me, bury and forget everything that he had done to me, and move on. That's what I convinced myself of. There are no winners, per se, in this story, but at this point he definitely had the upper hand.

Through complications spanning from my mindset shift, Sarah and I broke up. I had only one goal now, and that was to get away from everything. School, home, and everyone I knew – I wanted to be rid of it all. Back in the boarding house I couldn't sleep at night; when the world was quiet the disquiet raged inside my head. It was like feeling an incredible rage but not being able to identify a reason for it. I knew what Ernest had done to me, but I had convinced myself that what he did wasn't that bad, that it could be justified and surely couldn't be the reason for the anger I felt. I was beginning to move past denial; to repress my memories, burying them even further down to the point where I wouldn't recall them for more than a few moments at a time. Even then it would be a fleeting recollection, like a short-lived glimpse into a nightmare, usually occurring at times when I was feeling very low. But there was no reprieve from the anger I felt. It stayed with me, festering and rotting me from the inside.

Repressing my memories was an involuntary response to protect myself from the ongoing pyschological trauma I was experiencing. Whilst I was never entirely free of them or the mental images they evoked, they were no longer explicitly present in my mind. At times it was as if they had never happened, so that I was unable to associate my looming sense of loathing with them. This only made the abuse all the more damaging for me. I still bore the sense of turmoil that accompanied my molestation, but now in the absence of a definable catalyst my sense of perpetual angst only worsened, with added consternation.

I have mentioned my boarding school brushes with alcohol, drinking whenever the opportunity presented itself. Now I began devoting my free time to looking for it. My previous methods of escaping from reality were lost to me, so I needed something else to take the edge off reality. For the most part there was never enough alcohol to have any great effect on me – usually only a few cans of beer or cider, shared amongst those responsible for sourcing them. Soon I stopped chasing the buzz from drinking and became solely interested in the exhilaration of knowing I might get caught. Before long I got my wish. Students got caught all the time, and would happily grass up other kids they were drinking with in an attempt to dodge or reduce their punishment. My name got mentioned quite frequently, so I was later informed.

One particular evening I'd chosen to share a bottle of cider with a girl who was having a rough time. We weren't alone, some of her friends were with her; but I'd helped get the bottle, so I drank what I wanted and left them to it. Under the supervision of her friends she proceeded to get completely inebriated. We'd purchased a two-litre bottle of Strongbow, I hadn't drunk that much of it and her friends weren't partaking, yet apparently the bottle was entirely consumed. Poor girl. Anyway, she'd been dragged back to her boarding house where she was intercepted by the on-duty teacher, and her friends were very quick to lay the blame at my feet. As my name featured frequently in such tales, this was enough to drag me in front of my house master, who demanded that I tell him everything. I seem to remember telling him almost nothing other than that I didn't really care, and maybe that I was sorry. That landed me in the headmaster's office the following day, where I was informed that I was to be suspended. My parents would be contacted and needed to pick me up by the end of the day. Of course, Ernest's cell phone number was the only contact number they had for my parents. A letter formalising my suspension would be sent home in due course, my address was on file, my Mum would soon be finding out about my extracurricular activities and would surely start wondering why I was behaving in such a repugnant and obnoxious manner.

My exhilaration had peaked and worn off. The problem with the thrill of the chase is that once you get caught it vanishes rapidly. I didn't care that I was getting suspended – being at school was an exercise in futility – but I didn't want to go home. I was doing my utmost to bury and move past everything that had happened, but I still couldn't reconcile the ideas of being happy and going home; home still didn't seem like a safe place to me. As it happened, someone else didn't want me returning home under these circumstances either. Of course Ernest wouldn't want the news that I was a regular drinker at school or that I was being suspended getting around. If my wider family found out they would start asking questions, and my Mum would certainly start to query whatever manipulation he had stifled her with. No, he couldn't have that.

Apparently, Ernest could move quickly when placed under pressure; he used his position in the Army to secure himself a barrack room at the military camp where he worked, for a few days. I don't know under what pretence he managed this; I would see out my suspension there before he dropped me back to school. As far as the letter went, I don't know if it was sent home and he intercepted it, whether he told the school faculty to give it to him in person, or whether he simply changed the postal address the school had on file – but it never saw the light of day. Short of my committing a serious crime or dropping dead, there was no way anyone else except Ernest was going to be contacted about what I would get up to at school.

In a sense it was liberating. There was nothing Ernest could do to punish me that would be any more nefarious or severe than what he had already done – and besides, I was over all that now. Or so I told myself. Those hideous acts he made me participate in were lost to yesterday and I had moved on. I'd see out this suspension, and once it was over, I was going to work out how to escape this life permanently.

CHAPTER NINE

Departure

TIME AND MEMORY commingle in a strange symbiotic relationship; personal recollection is a fickle practice at the best of times. When trying to retrieve a memory from the brain you rely on three different parts: the hippocampus, neo-cortex and the amygdala. Cruelly, children who are victims of abuse are susceptible to defects affecting various aspects of brain development, including that of the hippocampus and amygdala – the very areas of the brain those children may have to rely on later in life to testify to their abuse and seek justice. Fortunately for me, despite the best efforts of my unconscious mind during younger years, I can recall most events with a worrying degree of clarity. This is a testament to those people who have helped me during my recovery.

But I can't account for much of the time between that suspension and leaving school before sitting my AS levels. An entire year and a half of schooling has essentially slipped out of the reach of my memory; all I can do is inform you of some key events that took place, and a rough estimate of when they occurred.

Not long after returning from my suspension I began to reconnect with Clare. I would love to justify this as some solemn quest to be loved and accepted, but it wasn't, despite what I told myself at the time. In reality, my intentions were solely for personal gain: I wanted to recreate the fake reality I had her believing during our last interactions, and escape into it once more. Now with the suspension behind me and all the memories safely sunk in a sea of repression, a strange confidence and different personality started to emerge and fill the void left behind. Not a good confidence that grants you a commanding presence or the capacity to do the right thing in the face of adversity, but a toxic confidence – the type of confidence that lets you see an opportunity, identify those weaker than you, and practise manipulation. This state of mind was not a conscious decision, but all my sympathy and compassion had atrophied – likely the result of the imbalanced sea of norepinephrine, serotonin and dopamine raging inside my brain, further intensified by the lack of intervention by any concerned third party.

I still had Clare's number from our previous farce of a relationship, and now I set out to rekindle it. This time I promised her we would see more of each other. I kept my promise to her every weekend I needed to vacate the boarding house. This perceived effort on my behalf made Clare very fond of me, and we remained an item for the remainder of my stay in England.

The benefit to me of her being completely unconnected from my life up until this point was that she had no prior knowledge, outside of what I told her by text, of who I really was. I was free to assume a slightly more mature version of the character I had presented to her in the previous iteration of our relationship.

I had made a couple of closer 'friends' in recent months as well, though these friendships were not positive things. The basis of our friendship was, basically, behaving like assholes. One of them lived twenty minutes or so from the school, an excellent option for me if I was unable to visit Clare because I didn't have enough money for the train. On those weekends we would go to his house, drink, sneak onto the school ground and wreak general havoc. Two of the three of us developed a drug habit in the time we remained close. Remarkably, I wasn't one of them. I dabbled, given the opportunity, but general drunken waywardness and antics were release enough for me – perhaps a saving grace. Besides, climbing that 'anti-climb' paint wall to get into the school was hard enough without being drunk and high. We were somehow never caught during any of the shenanigans we carried out during the last of our time at school; but we quickly developed a reputation for misbehaving as a group, resulting in our being banned from attending our school prom in the final year – even before it was announced. I think we all preferred it that way. Those two would eventually leave to attend other schools for their A levels.

There were times in this period when I returned home, but there is virtually nothing that I can recall to write about here; I just know I couldn't have avoided it completely. I can recall one weekend when I was collected from school because of my GCSE coursework. Whilst entirely uninterested in achieving anything academic, completing coursework to the minimum standard was preferable to having my free time taken away from me in the form of detention. I was taking music as a subject; I was actually quite good at it, but the coursework for GCSE requires a level of composition in a specific genre, so you had to be awake and paying attention in the classes. There was no way I was going to complete that piece of work, let alone achieve any kind of passable standard, and since it represented a majority of the GCSE grade, I was going to fail.

This must have been communicated to my parents via a letter or phone call, which of course only Ernest received. This is a safe assumption because though I certainly didn't say anything, he demanded my coursework and spent the rest of the weekend completing it on my behalf – a far better use of his time than what he would have preferred to be doing with me, in my opinion. For a long while I struggled to fathom why he did this. I was no longer of the mindset that he loved me; I had buried that crap deep down with my old personality which was still alive down there somewhere. Could it have been an attempt at reconciliation? No. The actual answer is obvious, and it's consistent with his previous behaviour. If a child fails a GCSE, people find out and start asking questions. Ernest was not prepared for me to be asked those questions, let alone answer them, so he took over and made sure I passed, (Sorry, whoever marked that coursework.) I can't recall enough detail from any one specific event to describe the abuse I received during this period of time. It occurred and I continued to pretend it didn't; testament to the brain's power to repress memories and dissociate.

Year Eleven was the final year of my GCSE. I passed, just barely. I spent the majority of my exam time asleep on my examination desk in the gymnasium, with the entire year group sitting their exams around me. Not a good look, but it was much easier to rest amongst the dull hum of pencils scratching on paper punctuated by the occasional cough or snort, than in the eerie disquiet of my mind at night. I can remember my Mum being so happy that I passed and saying she was proud of me and my grades, which were clearly below average.

If anything, continuing to function at a basic level was something worth celebrating at this point. Mum was still unaware of my abuse, so she must have just blamed my grades on my learning difficulty, and I was happy to accept praise where it was given without protest. I had already agreed, after some battling, to sit A levels at the same school. I had not given up on the idea of shedding that life though; I still plotted to escape.

I returned for my twelfth year of school, the AS levels. I was now seventeen years old, three years since I was first molested by my stepfather. I had no intention of seeing out that year. Despite my best efforts, I could not formulate a reasonable plan to execute my release from the education system and into society. Of course I wasn't ready, either; but I didn't know that, and wouldn't have accepted the advice anyway. Clare lived a few hours away from my school, and well away from my own home. Moving in with her always seemed like a good option, if I could find a way to make it work. Whilst uninterested in my parents' opinions, I wanted to avoid an all-out fight that might unearth things I would rather keep buried. Just not turning up to school one day and proclaiming I had left home to live with my girlfriend would certainly have that effect. There would need to be some kind of agreement made.

Lo and behold, not long after the school year started Ernest and my Mum decided they were up and moving to New Zealand with my brothers and me – just selling up and doing it without a plan. There's something brave about that ... and a few other things. Immediately I rejected the notion that I would join them. If he was going to leave the country, I wasn't stupid enough to follow him –this was an unbelievable opportunity for me. I wanted to avoid confrontation if I could, and I doubted Ernest would protest too much if I dug my heels in and refused to go; I was getting older now, so he was probably getting bored with me, anyway. I was fairly sure my Mum would have different ideas, though.

Over time they divulged more of their plan. It involved my Mum heading out to New Zealand six weeks prior to the rest of the family joining her, as she would need to buy a house for the family to move into once everyone arrived. She had managed to find employment through an agency, and would take on the role of breadwinner whilst Ernest planned to give up work. It got better: Ernest had to release from the Army and hand over all the projects he had been on recently, which would mean spending those six weeks away from the house. Someone, an au pair my parents told me, would need to move in to look after my brothers when they began to put this plan of theirs into motion. This would obviously be a paid position, and I set my sights on it. If I could get all my ducks in a row – have somewhere to live once my family left the country and get six weeks earning behind me – I felt I would have as good a chance as any of making it by myself.

All I needed to do was free myself from school in time to take up the au pair position. As they had inadvertently given me ample opportunity to prepare, I began to enact my plan.

If you and I were to meet on the street and you were to ask what subjects I studied for my A levels, I could not tell you. I know I took photography for a while; I've always enjoyed the more creative disciplines, even though I was not blessed with a knack for them. Other than that, I just don't remember. I only attended a term of my AS levels before making the final decision that I was going to drop out. I fully intended to make myself available for the au pair position, and this way the timing would be perfect.

My Mum didn't get the news initially when I decided I was not going to continue schooling, because Ernest had all my school correspondence redirected, but I told her eventually; she was livid. She had intended for me to finish my A levels. She thought I could stay at the boarding school, then with family when school wasn't an option, in order to complete my education. 'Livid', 'distraught' and 'infuriated' are the best words I can come up with to describe how she reacted. My Mum did want the best for me and, in the absence of this book to catch her up on the events I had endured over the last few years, she would not understand my decision. But a decision it was, and the decision was made. Lacking a better option, and given the opportunity to save some money, my Mother and Ernest agreed to let me take up the au pair position.

I hadn't attended any of my classes that year, except for photography, and that continued. Kids at school had many more free periods during A levels, intended for study, used for leisure. This meant I was generally in the company of at least a small group as I spent the last of my school days reclining in the common room, watching TV without a care in the world. All this while I have been talking solely about myself; however, the relationship I had been fostering with Clare, who lived in the Birmingham area, was blooming. She was head over heels for me – personally I don't know why, but she was. Everything I had been doing to garner her affections and keep her interested had worked a charm – so well, in fact, that my charm rubbed off on her family too; when asked, they agreed to have me live with them when my family left the country. I had met them in person a few times, so this new personality I was wearing around, like a very comfortable and well-fitting mask, must have made a good impression on them. It was incredibly kind of them to have me; I didn't properly acknowledge this at the time.

In case you thought I had shared my plan openly with my family – I hadn't. This was for me to know and them to find out. So if you're wondering how I managed to feel so relaxed whilst the clock ticked down to my family's departure and my impending homelessness, it's because I had it all worked out, or so I thought.

The day came; Mum embarked on the first chapter of her new life in New Zealand; I packed up my dorm room and came home by train. Ernest didn't pick me up this time, having made his way to an Army camp hours away from our house to carry out a few weeks of handover. All the while, my brothers were are at home feeling incredibly confused, perhaps even frightened. I should have been significantly more empathetic with them. I had been them not all that long ago, and I knew how poorly my parents handled tough situations. I was not present when the move was explained to them or how the next six weeks would work, but I can imagine how dull and factual it would have been, while also lacking key details. My brothers would have understood they were leaving the country, and I suspect that was it. They wouldn't appreciate that their friends would change, the culture would change, the TV shows they enjoyed would no longer be there. The family members who visited us, going for Christmas with my Uncle Anthony ... that would all stop. These are all things that as adults we can skim from a fact-based conversation. Children have to be told these things repeatedly and have them conveyed through stories in order to properly comprehend them. They need reassurance and guidance from parental figures in order to feel secure. My brothers were left in limbo as their parental figures did their own thing. Nor could they have understood when I didn't leave for New Zealand with them; I should have explained it to them, but I didn't. Those six weeks passed, and I shirked my responsibilities to my brothers and essentially left them to fend for themselves. I am not proud of that. I was too pre-occupied with escaping into my online world and manipulating my girlfriend into thinking I was someone else.

At the end of the six weeks we made our way to the airport. All four of us walked up to the check-in counter and joined the queue. I knew Clare and her family were outside waiting for me; I knew that in the next ten minutes I would be rid of this life that was causing me so much torment and strife. Free to live as I pleased. Then the sinking feeling came; in the next ten minutes my baby brothers would be lost to me. My Mum who I had treated so poorly, who had done nothing but try and love me, gone. It hurt me to see my brothers standing there with their regular-sized bags on their backs swamping their small frames. My brothers standing there, with his arms over each of their shoulders. That figure standing between them, in front of me was the reason I was having to leave. I stood in that line as the realisation dawned on me: I loved my family, I didn't want to leave them, I just wanted him to go away. I wanted Ernest to suffer like I did –why did I have to leave like this? *He* should be the one to be exiled! Not me! Repressed memories and unwanted thoughts erupted and dissipated like a brief clap of thunder in an otherwise mundane patch of rain. I was powerless to change anything, I knew that. I called to my brothers and said goodbye. They didn't understand; they looked to their father who offered no explanation, confused as they watched their older brother walk away.

CHAPTER TEN

Dawn of a New Failure

IN STARK CONTRAST to the confused and dismaying scene I had just departed, what awaited me outside the terminal was joy and excitement. I felt it too. Clare was ecstatic that I was coming home with her. Her grandfather, who drove, also seemed very optimistic about it all. I was very cautious around older authoritative males; I still am to this day – something I can be forgiven for, I think, given what you now know. I don't remember much of that journey other than holding Clare in my arms the whole way back to her house in Birmingham, thinking things couldn't get any better.

This entire chapter of my life is a hazy mess to me – not like before, not a fog hanging over my memory like a morning mist as a result of years of trauma and repression, no. This haze was solely self-inflicted. Have you ever been out partying for a couple of nights in a row, or more, and then struggle to recall even significant events? That's the haze I'm contending with here.

At this point in time, if you were to turn to me and say, "Holy shit you were naïve!", I would tend to agree. I was nearly eighteen, striking out by myself with the clothes on my back, bag slung over my shoulders, and a small amount of money in my account. I feel like at some point along my journey I was afforded an allowance for making mistakes. Obviously I had made a lot of mistakes on my way to this particular point, but I didn't perceive the consequences as being anything particularly grave. I let myself feel secure in the small amount of money I had in my account. I had never seen even that minuscule amount of money, and given the value of things I had wanted in the past, I figured that could last me at least six months. After a few weeks of paying rent and buying my own food, the gravity of my situation dawned. The rent was minimal given the size of the place and the number of people residing there, which was a saving grace. But it was clear my funds wouldn't last.

Clare seemed like a great person to me when she was my only option for escaping Ernest, but she had fewer prospects than me, and even less motivation to address her situation. Her life plan was to sign up for social welfare and wait for a council flat to become available for her to move into so she could get away from her Mum. Oh yeah, turned out that Clare hated her Mum, which became even more of an issue when they lived in a very small house immediately across the hall from each other. I'm not trying to write off Clare or her family as bad people; they had huge hearts. Letting me into their home was an incredible kindness, and they were never unkind to me. I am simply trying to describe my realisation that escaping Ernest was not the only challenge that life presented. I had planned to spend six months goofing around and trying to enjoy my new life. But that was cut massively short upon being introduced to the cost of living. It was time to find a job! Let's not dwell on the job search. For argument's sake I'll ask you to accept that in a fairly short period of time I was able to secure reasonable employment. Once that box was ticked, things were really great for a while.

I had barely given a moment's thought to Ernest, my family or my childhood since we had gone our separate ways that day at the airport. I didn't hear from them either. I couldn't shake the anger and resentment that clung to me. Even though I was free of Ernest I still harboured an animosity stemming from his actions against me, though I still wasn't directing blame at him. All I could do to seek reprieve from the raging confusion was to distract myself. I did this by spending time with Clare, working on a new social life and just generally having fun. Then there was my day job, another great distraction from those less than happy thoughts I'd tried to abandon at the airport.

Anyone who has been through anything will tell you that simply not thinking about an issue and ignoring it is not a healthy way to deal with it; repression is not conducive to recovery. If you get a cut and don't clean it out, it's going to get infected. If you don't act against that infection, it's going to spread and spread until you either have to take drastic action with far more dire consequences, or die. But for the time being, I was happy just ignoring the cut and letting it fester. Hanging out with friends, spending time with Clare, not having to sneak around to smoke cigarettes, drinking when I felt like it and earning my own money was all I needed; until it wasn't enough. After a short while it became clear that the small amount of money I was paid on a monthly basis would not be enough to lead any kind of life beyond drinking and smoking, even with the cheap rent available due to living in Clare's Mum's house (which was shared by Clare's Mum, Clare, me, Clare's younger sister and her partner, who was my age). Clare's sister's partner was called Steve; Steve may have been in the same position as me, I don't presume to know. He actually lived locally and had a home, but very seldom stayed there.

During my stay in Birmingham I became acquainted with people who were quite proud of not working at all. Many of these people received various social welfare payments and were in a better financial position than me, with their own flats. I was beginning to better understand the world Clare had come from, and why her bar for life was set so low. I wasn't ready to resign myself to that yet. It seemed appealing at times, but I was sure I could work out something better. I spoke to my employers about taking on more hours, and they obliged. I now had almost a full work schedule starting at reasonable hours, around six in the morning. What the average person would call reasonable hours of the morning were not, in my opinion at the time, reasonable hours. I would also not be capable of maintaining a schedule of "reasonable hours" for very long. I had the notion in my head that all was well, that now I was free of Ernest there would be no further strife in my life. Complete denial, of course. I was still partaking in all the same shit I got up to in school, the only difference being that I didn't have to sneak around. Things weren't actually any better – on the contrary, they were in quite a rapid state of decay, I just couldn't see it. All I had ever told myself was that a world without Ernest was a perfect world. I suppose once you've mastered denial it's easy to view any situation through that lens.

Whilst I struggled along, my Mum got in contact with me, via what must have been a very expensive phone call. She had secured a flexi ticket that I could use within twelve months if I wanted to come and visit. She referred to it as a holiday. I had no intention of ever using it, but it was easy to be courteous and grateful over the phone.

Months rolled by and somehow I remained employed, managing to make it to work in time for my shifts by the skin of my teeth. My body was not holding up well against the lifestyle I was subjecting it to. I was self-medicating with cigarettes, booze and food – not that I knew that at the time – part of my cycle of self-abuse now that I was responsible for my own wellbeing. The food was unintentional; I had no ability to prepare food at the time, and Clare was fond of the local bakery and McDonalds. Both were cheap establishments that we frequently visited, offering foods that grant quick gratification but should never become staples of anyone's diet. The evenings became later and later affairs, as both Clare's and my social circles became larger and larger. Circles full of people who, as previously mentioned, were not going places in life. At the end of the evening's festivities, which by then would generally have devolved into morning activities, Clare and I would saunter about town. We had both grown fond of this particular milkshake that we would go and buy in huge quantities at the local twenty-four-seven supermarkets, before wearily dragging ourselves home. Days when I didn't work would be spent in bed with Clare, sleeping off the previous night. When I had to work I would roll in, likely stinking of whatever had gone on the previous evening, and inflict my presence upon all those around me. Just like when I was at school. Déjà vu, anyone?

Clare, being my age but unemployed, was struggling with the Job Centre. They couldn't credit that someone her age, with no history of trauma or disability, who had attended school, was unable to work. But that is exactly what she was telling them, and they were not going to stand for it. Clare would need to attend a course of her choosing at the community college and acquire work skills, or her social welfare payments would cease. After what can only be described as a fit of juvenile rage (another trait I did not know Clare possessed), she accepted what she was being told and enrolled in the first available class presented to her. Hairdressing. This was actually a great thing for Clare; I had had my work during the day, and then if there was a party or gathering in the evenings, we would go to that. This meant that, whilst not productive, I was kept pretty busy. Clare, on the other hand, never had anything on during the day, and as a result was neither productive nor busy, which made her incredibly bored and irritable. Soon after moving in with her I began to bear the brunt of those irritations. Attending college, although reluctantly, broke up the monotony and gave her something to do with her days.

There were no other changes as a result of Clare's job centre-driven training though, other than a little bit more money in her pocket each week from increased social welfare. So we continued life as it was, but were able to drink and smoke a bit more, get a larger portion from whatever fast food outlet we were visiting – and if we happened to pass the supermarket, maybe a cheeky milkshake. Combine this fabulously healthy lifestyle with no sleep and a fairly sedentary job, and you only end up one way – fatter. Clare somehow remained the same, I don't know how. I have a basic understanding of calories in versus calories out and the effect that has on the human body; she remains an enigma to me. I, on the other hand, was not blessed with whatever voodoo magic prevented her petite frame from turning into a sack of jelly, and I began to do just that.

Winter came to the Midlands, and as the result of an argument (I am too embarrassed to tell you what about) I had been sleeping in the attic. There was a sleeping bag up there, and you could smoke because all the fumes would just go out through the tiles; there was no insulation to worry about setting alight. I didn't mind being up there one bit, except it was harder to squeeze through the hatch now to climb in. My shifts still started at six am, and with Christmas approaching in the UK my particular job was getting quite busy. We were expected not only to be on time but to actually perform the basic functions of our employment – heaven forbid. One evening I forgot my phone on the ground floor of the house. Consequently I had no alarm clock or way to tell the time, the nearest clock to me being on the floor below, mounted to the wall. Let me tell you now: sleeping in the attic of a uninsulated house during winter in the British Midlands does a lot of things to you, but it doesn't make you want to keep getting out of your warm sleeping bag, squeeze your unfamiliarly fat body through a hatch and down a ladder to check a clock that you have convinced yourself is still going to say midnight. As it happens, at the time I was having these thoughts it must have been about seven-thirty in the morning.

Alright, you squeezed my arm – I'll tell you why we argued. Clare and I had thrown down a multitude of times in increasingly fiery fights. This particular argument didn't go that way. As I've told you, Clare was training to be a hairdresser. She and I are no longer in contact, so I have no idea what she is up to now, but I wouldn't be surprised if she fulfilled her aspirations of doing sweet fuck all. I can tell you now, she certainly won't have become a hairdresser. As part of her course, she needed to practise a cut on a live model. She had been practising on this silly manikin for weeks, so when she asked me if she could practise some techniques on my then-long hair, I was happy to oblige. So we sat in the lounge; she pulled out her government-funded case full of various scissors and went to work. Fast forward fifteen minutes, and I looked like Michael Keaton's Beetlejuice. Much to her distaste, I told her as much. In hindsight, giving a somewhat unstable individual who is standing behind you clutching scissors less than constructive feedback probably wasn't my smartest move ever. Anyhow, things unfolded from there. So that is why I was sleeping in the attic. And on this particular morning, when I started hearing cars on the street starting up like they did just before their owners left for work, my tubby body and shit hair cut came rocketing down that attic ladder like a booger being fired from a nostril. I was still getting dressed as I made my way out the front door – I don't know if I was pulling shoes on or still buttoning up a shirt.

When I got to work I knew I was in for it. My manager expressed his anger and disappointment in my performance and lack of punctuality – for some reason he felt I was capable of more. As with all things when you can see them slipping away from you, I realised I was lucky to have had that job and really should have done better. I felt dismayed and ashamed of myself. I acknowledged I had let my manager down, as his harsh but true words fell upon my ears. I just felt bad all over, like a painfully hot rain falling all over me. I was ready to accept all the telling off and reprimanding or firing he was prepared to do, even beg for another chance. Then he threatened me. I didn't see that coming. He threatened physical violence against me for being late (and looking like a fucking cartoon character).

I have never been assertive. At the time I was confident in certain situations and knew I could play people, and when my mind was in the right place I found it easy to make people laugh – but assertiveness was not a strong point. In times of confrontation, if I was not completely certain that I was right I would accept blame and move on, it's just easier. This was different, though. I had just been physically threatened for something I had done, but I wasn't going to accept his violent threats. In another near out-of-body experience like the one I had the first night Ernest came into my room and started this long story of abuse instead of simply explaining the birds and the bees to his stepson, I watched myself brace up, plant my feet, lean forward and lock eyes with him. Was I going to punch him? That wouldn't work out well; there were cameras all over the place. Was I going to demand an apology? That would be fruitless ... No, I stared him in the eyes and told him to "Get fucked!", then I removed my work shirt and dropped it before leaving.

I don't know who had just told my manager to get fucked, but it wasn't me. As I walked home I slipped back into my body; my manager called me and said that I could come back if I wanted a second chance, but I immediately declined. That experience rocked me; I had yet again been just a member of the audience watching my own actions, wondering what would happen next as someone else piloted my body. I stormed home, going over the events that had just occurred as well as the decisions I'd made and the actions I'd taken that had led me to this point.

When I left my brothers at the terminal I thought I was freeing myself of Ernest and everything he'd done to me. Any thought of lingering issues or damage done to my brain had not entered my mind. But when my manager threatened me, I felt exactly as I had that night Ernest first revealed himself as a child abuser. I didn't realise it in the moment, but my fight-or-flight had kicked in; I'd been ejected from the driver's seat, becoming a passenger in my own consciousness. The fight-or-flight instinct took action to defend me against the perceived threat, this time manifested as my manager. It was the same part of my brain that had decided that I wouldn't be able to fight off or escape Ernest, rendering me still and dissociated all those years ago. Even though this time around I had come out of the encounter without suffering, I felt those same feelings of hopelessness for the first time in months. I was thinking about what Ernest did to me, the repressed memories were bubbling up out of the swamp of repression I had buried them in, and I couldn't shove them down fast enough. I was in turmoil. I could feel so much hate, yet I had nowhere to direct it; it was just a massive ball of seething angry fire that I couldn't contend with. The idea of allocating blame didn't even occur to me. I knew Ernest had done those things to me, but all this pain I was grappling with seemed unrelated. I was angry and just so confused.

Still on my way home, now irate and enmeshed in a dark cloud of emotion, I was distracted from the storm in my mind by my reflection in a passing shop window. I wouldn't normally have paid any heed – perhaps it was my mood, or the fact that I didn't have a larger overcoat or jacket on top of my t-shirt – but I saw myself, and I didn't recognise the reflection. I was a mess. It was just a short stop, only long enough to be plausibly perusing items in the window, when in actual fact I was just reaffirming what I had seen – an utter disgrace. First, that haircut that may well have been the catalyst for all of this; then there was my face, eyes all bloodshot from lack of sleep and bloated cheeks from a diet of salt and alcohol. As I lowered my gaze I took note of my body too. I knew that I wasn't as lean as I once had been, but looking at myself now, all I saw was a sack of shit: bad posture, sloping shoulders that were narrower than my now wide mid-section, complete with a gut hanging just above it. Until that moment I'd been pretty sure that this life in Birmingham was all working out; very quickly that delusion shattered around me. The situation I was in just stank, and it was my own fault. I had altered my personality to manipulate Clare into liking me so I could escape Ernest, but in doing so I had sacrificed my wellbeing and sense of self entirely; I had been temporarily happy living under the delusional idea that I was content just to be rid of him, but I wasn't. This wasn't me; something needed to change.

When Clare got home from her hairdressing course, I imparted the news of my day to her; she didn't seem phased.

Unemployment was normality to her, perhaps even a preferable fate to that of the working professional. In my naivety (yes, I admit it), perhaps coupled with my inability to assign Ernest any blame for my situation, I felt that my appearance was the problem. I could acknowledge that I hadn't adequately met my employer's expectations, but blind in the face of truth, I blamed what had happened on my self-image. I had heard the tropes: that you need to dress for the job you want, not the job you have, that if you look good you will feel good. Well I felt bad, and the obvious and easy solution to all this would be to get into shape and sort out this damn haircut. The haircut was a given anyway, but you catch my drift. I had a PhD in denial, and I could apply it to anything: "Re-experiencing dissociation during conflict, temporarily revisited by repressed memories of abuse and struggling with a sense of imminent doom? Must just be an image problem", I told myself. That night I abstained from the usual helpings of shit food in polystyrene boxes and went to the supermarket, where I would usually load up on milkshakes. I still did that, but also came home armed with some 'healthy' (better than McDonalds) options. I didn't drink alcohol that night, though I did still smoke. I stayed up late, but didn't party; I shaved off what was left of my hair from Clare's efforts the previous night; I looked different.

Slowly, over a few weeks, I made some progress towards losing weight and started feeling a little better. Fortunately I am my own biggest critic, so the obese mess I had witnessed in the shop window that day was probably only indicative of a few kilograms gained; but the impact it had on me was enormous. I started running, and cut down significantly on the shit food I had been eating – partly due to no longer being employed and having to make jobseeker allowance stretch further; partly through a developing personal discipline. Clare's Mum had also gotten an internet plan, so we had connectivity in the house. I used this to start reading, in the hope that I might stumble across the secret to fixing my life and feeling better. In my search for deliverance from feeling like a fat failure, I came across the concept of Kaizen.

Kaizen is largely accepted as a business concept, but it has far reaching applications. Literally translated from Japanese, it means "change for better". Nowadays Kaizen is synonymous with continuous improvement, and is becoming more and more diluted as a concept. If you look you will frequently see the word 'Kaizen' thrown in with Six Sigma practices, because at their core they're very similar. I am not here to preach process improvement practices though, I'm talkin' bout brain stuff. When I first came across Kaizen the article communicated its message in a more philosophical manner than you might find in a continuous improvement article intended for a business. It suggested that I should place more emphasis on the process of getting to a destination rather than the outcome itself. The article suggested I identify small problems and address them immediately, eventually adding up to a large-scale fix, rather than trying to tackle the entire problem all at once. Given the small changes I had been making in my life and the success I was having with them, I saw value in this. It's a principle I have since tried to adopt each and every day. A Youtuber I watched one evening stated that the art of Kaizen is to get one percent better each day; he wouldn't be entirely correct, but the concept is sound. I didn't need to fix everything overnight, I just needed to get a little better each day.

So I continued what I was doing. I was feeling much better about myself. Concurrently, Clare became more and more bitter towards me, likely because I was being more like myself rather than wearing that mask, that other fictional personality. Despite not acknowledging the existence of my repressed memories, accepting my abuse or dealing with the fact that I was unable to allocate blame to Ernest for anything he had done to me, I began to restore a sense of self-worth by engaging in practices that made me feel more like myself than I had done since the night he ruined my life.

My eighteenth birthday had been and gone by this point. Due to the limited messaging I had sent out about my new home location, few people actually knew where I was. More diligent and concerned family members were able to get that information without too much trouble by talking with my Mum – including my grandparents, who sought my whereabouts on behalf of my biological father. A card arrived for me from him, with his phone number. We talked almost immediately after I received the card and arranged a time to meet. Nothing especially significant occurred during this visit other than to reaffirm that my father wanted to know me and wanted me in his life. I only visited my father's family for a day, but I enjoyed myself and their company; being with them was unlike anything I had experienced in recent years. The conversation didn't feel stilted or forced. I felt a sense of belonging, like we were family. I wasn't having to wear my mask or even thinking about altering my personality – it was liberating. I did, however, feel quite embarrassed at the sorry state of affairs my life was in. Seeing how they lived and the successes they were all enjoying collectively and individually did make me feel like more of a failure – not something that they should be criticised for at all. In fact, seeing that I shared genetics with successful and honest people only stoked the fire that was slowly starting to ignite under me, urging me to sort my life out. I would have liked to have spent much longer there and gotten to know my father, stepmother and brothers again; to have asked for advice on what I should do with myself. But there isn't time in a single day. When my Dad dropped me at the train station to return to Clare I intended to return, to reconnect with him and my family. But the powerful undertow of life would soon separate us again.

Upon my return to Birmingham Clare was waiting, same as ever, not entirely impressed with the person I was striving to become. She wanted a comfortable life, and aspired for very little. The Alex who had grown increasingly lazy and fat whilst accompanying her to various fast food outlets and parties, who worked a dead-end job just to buy booze and cigarettes, could fit into that life. The Alex who was now trying to prepare healthier meals in the kitchen, not boozing every night, and heading out for runs when possible, could not be a part of it. Our two trajectories were no longer conducive to each other. She would have been happy if I had let myself go to the point of no return, so that I would always be there to keep her company and entertain her, but that was not a life I wanted any part of. There was a decision to be made.

I am making Clare out to be an antagonist in my story, but that is not the case. I had manipulated Clare into believing I was someone that I was not. I designed and wore a mask over my personality, knowing that she would like what she saw. Now I was choosing not to wear it, I was choosing to be myself, someone she didn't know or like. Clare wanted the Alex she knew to stay. She is not the bad guy here; it was I who weaselled my way into her life under false pretences, and it was I causing the upset now as I tried to find a way to manipulate the situation to better suit my purposes. Clare was happy in complacency; I should have just left her be.

I have asked myself time and time again how I could have justified my behaviour towards Clare. I was carrying out a despicable, unforgivable deceit. When I decided to carry out my plan to escape Ernest all I saw was a way out; I didn't think of the harm I would do other people. It was a singleminded, selfish act. Yet I carried on my deception day in, day out, without remorse. It became habit. I was cued to adopt my character, to wear my mask, when I saw Clare. She represented my freedom from Ernest, and that was all the motivation I needed to be whoever I needed to be and to play my role without a second thought. My acts were rewarded by her affection and acceptance of me, which only added to the reserves of ammunition I was stockpiling to convince myself that I was happy living this lie. And thus the loop was completed: cue, routine and reward; and I was primed to do it all again, a sphere spinning in perpetual motion, until it was interrupted by the conflict with my manager.

I had been looking for work – maybe not as diligently as I could, but I was looking, and nothing was turning up. I had thrown away my last job through sheer complacency, and was growing angry with myself for making such a rash decision. I was looking for a job, and as far as I could tell, there was nothing to be had. My relationship with Clare was becoming more and more sour every day, and the living situation was becoming intolerable, all whilst showing no signs of improving. I had tasted the life that was here for me in the British Midlands, and it tasted awful. I had a flexi ticket to New Zealand that was soon expiring; the decision needed to be made. My family was out there, my Mum and brothers who I loved and missed – but Ernest was also in New Zealand. I had been looking at New Zealand online now that I could, and it looked beautiful. Living there would be an amazing opportunity, and staying in Birmingham was no longer an option, but ... Ernest was in New Zealand. I had a newfound relationship with my Dad's family, perhaps they would take me in. Looking back now I know they would have, but at the time I talked myself out of it, the headspace I was in persuading me that they would see me as a disgrace. I went around and around in my head, but any reasonable line of thinking about leaving the UK met the same roadblock. Ernest was in New Zealand; he was the obstacle. I still didn't hate him – that big ball of hate on my walk home from quitting my job had been doused in water and buried again, because I didn't know what to do with it. A part of me, that I was holding underwater so I couldn't speak, knew he had abused me; that didn't mean I could allocate him blame for it. I couldn't resolve the decision by myself, so I turned to the only person I had to talk to.

I spoke with Clare at length about New Zealand, and she was surprisingly collected and rational throughout. In the end we agreed I should go to New Zealand for a holiday, test the waters, and come back. Maybe we would both go out together at a later date. So I called Mum. For someone who had been on the receiving end of so much verbal flak from me, she was elated when I told her I'd be using the ticket, even if it wasn't to stay permanently. Back in the UK I packed up a bag and prepared for my trip. Passport in hand I was ready to go. I shared the news with my Dad, but I didn't elaborate too much; he knew some of my living situation and agreed that New Zealand sounded like a good option. He wanted to see me again, to wish me well before I left, but it turned out not to be possible.

My Uncle Anthony came to collect me from Clare's house – this man who had once been such a pivotal figure in my life, the man who I would later realise was my most important role model. When faced with difficult decisions or morally conflicted situations I often paused to ponder, "What would Anthony do?" Well, I can tell you that he wouldn't have allowed himself to end up in the situation that I had landed in; but if he was presented with the option of doing nothing or taking action to seek a better life in New Zealand, he would act.

Uncle Anthony knew full well everything I had done from my family's perspective. I'd been utterly vile to my mother, rude and neglectful of my family; I'd wasted my youth playing games, I perpetually stank of cigarettes, I'd been generally worthless and dropped out of school to leave home early. He knew all of this about me, yet when he turned up there to take me to the airport it was just like those Sundays when he would take me to hockey. He pulled up to the house and opened up the boot. Smiling as he did, he walked up to me with his hand held out in front and shook mine firmly, telling me it was good to see me. He helped me with my bags into the car and drove me to the airport. He didn't mention what a stupid idea not going to New Zealand in the first place was. He didn't criticise anything I had done or hadn't done, just asked me how I was and talked to me like a human being. It was a lovely car journey.

Once at the airport he helped me check in and bought me lunch. Anthony knew Pizza Express was my favourite; when I was allowed to see my Dad, before the events in Sandhurst, that's the restaurant he would take me to. Uncle Anthony bought and shared Pizza Express with me for lunch and then told me he was proud of me; he said he saw the positives in me making decisions for myself, and hoped I enjoyed my trip to New Zealand. Soon it was time to go through security; we said our goodbyes, and I told him I would see him when I got back. He smiled, nodded his head and waved. I was happy as I made my way through security, waving until I lost sight of him going through the security gate. I loved that man; he had no reason to be kind to me, yet he was. He was never judgemental or gave his opinion where it wasn't warranted, yet when he gave advice everyone listened. He supported me when he didn't have to, and showed me how to be a man. Without wanting to be hyperbolic, without his influence in my life I can promise you I wouldn't be here today.

My Uncle Anthony doesn't get much of a mention in my book, and that's because a lot of my book is about bad shit in the world – there's just so much bad shit. My Uncle Anthony was everything that was good in the world, and the shining light of his example was so bright he didn't even need to be present for me to feel it. I loved my Uncle Anthony, and that last wave I gave before losing sight of him as I walked through the security gates would be the last time I ever saw him.

CHAPTER ELEVEN

The Land of the Long White Cloud

THIRTY-SIX HOURS OF air travel and layovers combined is pretty arduous, but I got through it. What a trooper. Eventually I arrived at the intended provincial airport, New Plymouth, to be greeted by my family – with mixed emotions. On the surface, I was happy. I was genuinely happy to see my brothers, and to an extent my Mum. I still loved her, but because I also harboured resentment towards her, it was difficult to properly express that love. The happiness I felt to see her was stifled by other feelings.

Those other feelings were my unresolved issues with Ernest. He was there, and upon seeing him that ball of hate began to rise. I couldn't make sense of why – it seemed to exist only to confuse and upset me: "He did those things to you, but he was unwell, he loved you. He wouldn't do that again!" Parts of my brain were stretched thin trying to work through the signals ricocheting through my synapses which repression would not allow me to properly acknowledge. I wrestled that raging ball of hatred back down. There were embraces with varying levels of sincerity all round, followed by awkward small talk as we waited for my luggage. I had been absent from the family for over a year, choosing to leave them behind and embark on a journey of my own. The wheels had clearly fallen off my wagon whilst on that journey, though I don't know if anyone in my family knew that. Not a single question was asked about my time in Birmingham; they didn't ask, and I didn't tell. That's just how we handled things; we didn't have hard conversations.

That first encounter was awkward and cold. We attempted to express genuine warmth towards each other; most families would express such things without having to try. There was a dark presence in our family that prevented us doing so.

It was a fairly long drive back to the house my family had bought – over an hour in the car. I rode in the back seat with my brothers, Mum rode shotgun, and Ernest drove. There was little conversation during the journey, and perhaps fuelled by the silence, a sinister whisper started taunting me, reminding me that I was willingly returning myself to the prison he had kept me in. It wasn't a physical prison with tangible bars I could rattle, or manacles to chain me up. This was a metaphorical prison: the damage he had done to my psyche during the years of abuse was the cage holding me in; the thoughts he had implanted in my mind – that he loved me, or that my brothers and Mum would have to live without him if I told anyone – were the shackles that kept me in a corner. I couldn't see Ernest's face, only his eyes in the rearview mirror; but I imagined his features all twisted up into a malevolent grin, gleeful as he transported his plaything back to its cell. A shroud closed in over my vision – for the rest of that drive I didn't see my family, only my tormentor.

The house my Mum and Ernest had bought in New Zealand was nice, much bigger than anywhere we had ever lived in the UK. The roads to get there were like country lanes back in England, but these were main roads in New Zealand. The house was situated in a small town in Taranaki; I got the impression that this was a very rural region, it seemed very quaint. That same whisper in my head reminded me of what Ernest had done to me, but at the same time urged me to forgive him, to accept that he didn't mean me any harm, that he had been unwell. The whispers were my own subconscious thoughts, and I did not reject these lies I was telling myself – but I had been free of him for so long, I couldn't allow myself to submit to him again, sick or not. I was especially worried as to how I might react if he tried.

Ernest did try again, that first evening I arrived in New Zealand, as soon as I was alone. I was walking to the room that was to be mine. It was early evening and I was jetlagged; we had shared a takeaway dinner as a family whilst watching TV, but soon after finishing I excused myself so I could sleep. As I left the lounge he excused himself also and made a move to follow me, I can't remember under what pretence; I think it may have been to check my heater was working, or to show me where the towels were if I wanted to shower. I didn't look back, but I could hear his footfall on the carpet behind me; a cold sweat started on my back and my hairs stood on end. He followed me to my room and shut the door behind us. I didn't turn around, I felt like I was made of ice – my skin felt so cold it hurt. I felt his hands around my waist as he tried to pull me closer. I was sickened by the action but didn't react or push him away, nor did I allow myself to move under his direction. I felt his hands on my hips; his grip was firm, and he pulled me towards him.

I turned to face Ernest and stepped back. I looked at him and found myself looking down – I was bigger than him now, clearly stronger too; the time I had been away had seen me abusing my body, but my efforts in recent months had rendered me fitter and stronger than before. He, on the other hand, had clearly spent his recent retirement from the military doing nothing. Probably looking at pictures of boys on the internet. I felt something come over me; though the actions I was taking were my own, I also felt as if I had been imbued with a new confidence. Even from this position of power I felt small; yet the small act of defiance I had shown by stepping back from his grasp was not what Ernest was expecting – this was clear from the look on his face. That look reaffirmed my confidence that had begun wavering as soon as I felt it, and I doubled down on my defiant stance.

I told him to leave my room, that I didn't want him here. It was clear he didn't intend to oblige; it was as if I could hear his thoughts furiously turning over, trying to work out how he could see his disgusting desires fulfilled. But he couldn't simply overpower me, and I wouldn't let myself be talked into anything. He turned and left, shutting the door quietly behind him. I got into bed as if nothing had happened. My acute stress response had intervened again, but unlike the first night Ernest molested me – and the countless times after – I did not freeze. When my manager had threatened me, I had opted to fight; this had given me the power to resist Ernest now, so that on this occasion I was in the driver's seat. Unfortunately that acute response faded when the perceived threat of Ernest left, and was replaced by the apologetic whispers. "He just missed me", "It was only a hug, that was all", "He was unwell, but he's ok now" … the cyclic messaging of self-denial went around in my head. I was too tired to fixate on anything; sleep came quickly that night.

The following morning – or it might have been midday by the time I was up …when I got out of bed, my Mum was in the kitchen with a card in her hand. It was opened; apparently Clare's Mum had sent it to her. I never saw the actual content of this card, and I'm not entirely convinced this wasn't some manipulation from Ernest's standpoint. But the card allegedly said something along the lines of, "It's been super cool having your loser son stay here with us, but if you could like, you know, tell him never to come back that would be cool and all. Kthxbye. Signed, Clare's Mum." Like I said, I don't know the actual content of the card but that's how it was put to me: Clare's Mum enjoyed having me stay but didn't want me to come back. That was going to make for an interesting chat with Clare when I got online tonight. Whilst there was internet at the house, the only PC was in the lounge, so I would have my conversation with her within earshot of my family.

The conversation with Clare didn't go well at all. The plan was for me to test the waters and come back to her. She may even have had hopes that a run-in with my family might see me regress to my old self. We didn't split up immediately, but our relationship rapidly disintegrated from that point. Initially we agreed she would come out to New Zealand if we could scrape the money together for a ticket. I found work easily and started sending money back to her. For the next few weeks I would work, come home, talk to Clare online at the family computer and send her money on paydays.

Ernest kept trying to sway me to sleep with him; he never physically put hands on me again, but would ask if he could stay with me in my room, or if I wanted a shoulder rub – or other questions with the intention of getting me alone. My acute stress response did not take over again when he was just talking, so I became quite adept at dodging his advances and explaining away to myself the anger that would follow.

My Dad sent me some money in lieu of my nineteenth birthday, which was either coming or going. I weighed up buying a car or laptop – the cars which were available in that price bracket were not good ,so I got the laptop and it served me well for many years. This also meant I no longer needed to use the family computer to talk with Clare or send money home; I could now do it all from the comfortable solitude of my room. The downside to this was that Ernest's advances increased now that I was spending more time behind closed doors. Every time he made a pass at me, which I would reject, the carousel of denial would start to crank up in my head, excusing his actions but bringing with it the fiery sphere of rage. I would send him away and spend whatever time was left in the evening suppressing the feelings I could not reconcile. That room in which I began to spend so much more time outside of work, did not have proper curtains – only blinds with a small gap that could be peered around at the edges, should you wish to. I knew that when I sent Ernest away, he would go out there and watch me through that gap.

At the time I didn't quite grasp just how grotesque an activity he was carrying out with his observations of me, so I just left him to it. The carousal of denial handled all the apologies for him leaving me confused and distorted, sometimes angry with myself, for causing all this upset for Ernest. I knew one thing though: I needed to get away. I needed to find somewhere else to live.

Trying to live with Clare, whilst it had worked in my favour for a while, had ultimately been a failure. I had disguised who I really was in order to gain her affection – so I could worm my way into her life. That had come back to bite me, in a way. Regardless, at this point in the story I was still sending Clare money – money sent with the intention of purchasing flights and arranging a visa of some description in New Zealand. But shortly I learned from Clare's younger sister, who reached out to me, that my money was simply being spent frivolously. To add insult to injury, Clare had also shacked up with someone else in my absence. I confronted Clare through the only method available and she admitted everything, told me she did it because she missed me, together with other tropes associated with cheating. We then broke up. That particular evening Ernest was hanging around like a bad smell, particularly persistent in his attempts to stay in my room. Like a vulture circling a dying animal, he must have overheard what was going on between Clare and myself and hoped I wouldn't have the mental fortitude to turn him away.

Breaking up with Clare, whilst not premeditated, was the right thing to do. At the time I had convinced myself we were staying together for good reason, but we weren't. I had never been myself around her, and she didn't actually like *me* as a person – she liked the person I had pretended to be. It wasn't fair on either of us. But as Clare made her exit from my life, I still had all the same problems as before, the most immediate being my need to get away from Ernest. I had been looking briefly at rentals I thought would be affordable when Clare arrived, if she contributed towards the cost (which I now realise was a pipe dream). I could seek out a flat with other roommates in the area, but I didn't even know where to start looking for that. I also wasn't fond of my job, and could easily see it going the same way as the job I had in England. I still had the Kaizen principles in my head; I needed to get better, to fix my issues and reach better outcomes. I needed my own place to live; I needed a better job.

Given my history so far, I had very few career prospects. My Mum had always hinted that I should join the Military in some capacity. It was familiar to her; Ernest had been in the Army, and we had other relatives who also served. There had been moments when I was living with Clare that joining the British Military seemed appealing. I had even thought perhaps the two of us would be able to move into Military accommodation together; obviously, that did not pan out. I had some very conflicted feelings about following in Ernest's footsteps, but I chose to ignore them and instead focused on the primary goal, leaving home. Through equal parts denial and successful advertising campaigns on behalf of the New Zealand Defence Force, I soon found myself filling out the online application to be considered for the New Zealand Army.

Not dissimilar to the fresh motivation I had felt when trying to better myself after the conflict with my manager in Birmingham, I felt a new sense of direction now that I had applied for the Army. I had a new target, a goal I could work towards, and it felt good. I started getting out of the house more often to run and train, as I felt I should when preparing for the Army. Ernest's advances became less frequent too; perhaps he was beginning to get the message that I was never going to let him abuse me again. The rage that had arisen whenever Ernest would threaten to remind me of the abhorrent torment he had inflicted, no longer surfaced. I was free to bury the memories and emotions associated with my abuse deep down in the dirt, next to those foul images I would repress whenever they flickered across my mind.

Self-improvement was high on my list now. I had applied to join the Army, but how was I going to convince them to actually hire me? I knew that I needed to be in shape, something I had been working on; some kind of record of education would be needed as well. I identified that my GCSE grades were not great, and sought to rectify that issue. In doing so, I learned that GCSEs couldn't be crosscredited directly into New Zealand's education system under NZQA, so I would need to start all over again. I searched local establishments where I could gain some kind of accreditation; there were plenty of local colleges that I could attend and gain a NCEA qualification in a matter of months if I enrolled full time. It was clear to me that furthering my very basic level of education would be far more beneficial to any future career prospects, Military or other, than continuing with my current employer. I resigned and began studying soon after.

The Defence Force soon sent me further applications to complete and assignments to complete, which I worked through when I wasn't at College. I also needed to up my exercise regime in order to pass the fitness tests required of me. I worked hard to achieve what I needed in order to succeed in joining the Defence Force, and successful I was. At nineteen years old I was striking out on my own again, for the third time now. First off was the tree in Aldershot, and then Birmingham. Third time lucky, right?

CHAPTER TWELVE

Regimented Denial

I WAS PROUD of myself for what I had achieved in being accepted into the Army – not a common feeling for me. In common with most Armies, there was a requirement to pass a basic training or All Arms Recruit Course, as the New Zealand Army calls it, held in Waiouru. I completed the recruit course to the required standard, and as my reward I was given a life of my own, away from my abuser – although at this time I still let myself believe that he was just an awkward, quirky old man who simply had perverted tendencies toward younger men; harmless, as long as you could avoid him.

My basic training began around the same time as winter. Over one hundred recruits, myself included, contended with the harsh elements associated with the colder season in the barren wasteland of Waiouru. I was under no illusion that the next sixteen weeks would likely be the most physically challenging I had ever experienced in my life. They would also turn out to be the most exhilarating and gratifying. I was instilled by the Military instructors with a sense of purpose and direction unlike anything I had experienced before. The Army challenged me to succeed, and I rose to it.

Those four months I endured in Waiouru were a rite of passage I had to complete before being accepted into the Military family. The experience of learning how to be a soldier was both fascinating and exciting: I learnt bushcraft, survival, how to fire rifles and detonate explosives. But despite the allure of carrying out such tasks for a living, not all the recruits made it through. Some recruits succumbed to injury, or dropped out through a lack of mental fortitude. They were discharged back to their home locations and old lives, free to do as they wished. There was no chance that I would allow myself to become like them; I would avoid the discomfort of home at all costs.

At a certain point during my basic training I experienced something altogether unexpected. Whilst I did not blame Ernest for what he did to me, I would frequently and involuntarily be reminded of my abuse in quiet moments, feeling loathing and shame. But over the course of basic training these episodes became less and less frequent, and then stopped altogether. It was as if, between the challenges I had to overcome on a daily basis and the sense of direction and purpose that was being implanted within me, I simply had no time for the demons of my past; they were imprisoned behind a wall built from the sheer determination I was exerting to succeed at what I was doing, and so were kept at bay – for now.

Basic training was definitely one of the most physically challenging things I had ever done – but it also turned out to be the most enjoyable as well. I enjoyed the regimented structure and discipline; it meant I didn't need to think for myself, or worry about making the right or wrong decision –

I was simply given instructions to carry out. This was soothing for an abused mind. Positivity of experiences aside, I also made some great friends. There's nothing quite like the fires of shared suffering to forge the bonds of friendship. Friendships tempered in those flames are strong enough to stand the tests of time.

Towards the end of 2010 I "marched out" after successfully completing my recruit course, alongside my fellow (once recruits, now) soldiers. I was posted to a company based in Linton Military Camp, along with a handful of other members of the same trade.

The military life seemed great: shared accommodation, but with private rooms; a good salary paid to me each fortnight; and outside of mandated duties, once work was finished for the day my time was completely my own. I was free of the middle-aged man trying to seduce me in my own home, and no longer had to hide a secret from my family. My disembodied tormentors were safely sealed away in a prison forged with bars of my own sense of self-worth, and I was free to be my own person. I had no need to wear a mask anymore, no need to alter my personality. This was a fresh start.

My recruiter for the Army had promised me and everyone else he was trying to sign up for the intake that the Military would offer us the opportunity to see parts of the world that would be shut off to us as mere civilians; I didn't bother telling him that I was only interested in escaping my abuser. I suspected the glorious yarn he was spinning, of epic adventure that awaited once we passed basic training, was nothing more than hyperbole. As it happened, though, he wasn't being entirely dishonest. By January 2011 I had visited the continent of Antarctica as a member of the ship offload team tasked with resupplying McMurdo base for the year. I couldn't believe my luck. I had a job, friends, a safe place to live, and was being afforded the opportunity to travel to incredibly remote places.

I was loving every minute of Army life in those early days; with my sinister internal monologue safely on mute for the time being, there was little to dampen my enjoyment. On basic training, every minute of your day is heavily structured and accounted for; this is not the case once you march out. While a high standard of personal discipline is still expected of you, it is left to your discretion how to maintain or neglect it. Though the learned discipline of basic training stays with all recruits for a while, it is slowly washed away by the inevitable tides of complacency. It is simply human nature to take the path of least resistance – we are lazy creatures, generally speaking. Unfortunately, complacency was the key that would unlock the cell where I had locked my demons away.

Those who have been even remotely associated with the Defence Force likely have stories to share from their times experiencing its notorious drinking culture. I am not here to make allegations about whether it is problematic or not – that is superfluous in the context of this story. I am simply stating, based on observation and experience, that it exists and is rampant. In Linton you could find a party in camp or the surrounding housing area any night of the week; there was always a cause to celebrate something: a promotion, completion of a course, a corps birthday or just the fact that it was Tuesday. If you wanted to drown your sorrows, you could find someone to share in that activity without too much expended effort. My peers and I who had recently been posted to Linton were invited to join in miscellaneous festivities regularly. It wasn't a malicious attempt at indoctrinating us into a harmful culture of binge drinking, it was a gesture of inclusiveness and acceptance. Drinking together is part of the Military culture, and we were being accepted. At first I was wary of it – I remembered all too well the difficulty I had got myself into regarding drinking around the time I lived with Clare, along with general neglect of my wellbeing, and I didn't want to reexperience that.

Time passed and I continued working hard at my day job, which was fairly mundane and completely pointless, unfortunately (unless you consider moving large objects from one side of a warehouse to the other and back again repeatedly, ad nauseum, to be constructive). I was bored, but I felt that by applying myself to my work I would be graced with further opportunities to travel. Despite the multiple opportunities for amazing adventure that my trade offered, the company was poorly managed and so had a very high attrition rate. However, the workload did not decrease to allow for the drop in manpower, so the opportunities to travel abroad just kept coming. There were so few people in the trade that there was no requirement to excel in order to be chosen. Soon I had visited several different military bases, islands, countries and continents, all whilst having done little to earn those opportunities. The same was true of my peers; we were being rewarded whether we worked hard or not. As such, the detrimental human tendency to become complacent began to take effect over time, in both myself and my peers. Where we would have been doing exercise or brushing up on trade skills in our own time, we would now play console games or drive into town for takeout and movies. Unfortunately for me, the comforting embrace of complacency lulled me into a false sense of security. My demons started occupying the vacant space in my mind previously occupied by constructive tasks. Like a violent contagion they spread quickly through my mind, and in the absence of a vigilant instructor barking orders, enforcing structure and routine, I had little chance of chaining them back into the confines of their cell. I began being visited by flashbacks and sinister internal dialogues once more.

So rapid was their return to power over me that I found myself spending entire evenings isolated in my barrack room reliving the trauma I suffered as a young boy, powerless to prevent it. These were far more vivid and violent than I had experienced at any point prior. Given the availability and general acceptance of heavy drinking, it didn't take long before I was taking a bottle of whiskey or rum to my barrack room every evening so I could calm the turbulent, dark waves crashing in my head. There were other avenues of distracting myself from my torment – socialising with friends would work for a time, but eventually everybody needs to sleep. Just as he had visited me in the night when everyone else had turned in, so now would my demons, waiting for me in the darkness each night, and I I was forced to turn to drink just to get some rest. Soon alcohol had become my sole coping mechanism. I was able to hide my drinking from the eyes of friends who might become concerned, under the guise of just wanting to have a good time; like I explained earlier, the

Army had a vibrant drinking culture that would allow me to drink myself into a stupor each night in the name of some inconsequential celebration of irrelevance. When the festivities inevitably ended, I simply returned to my room; if sleep eluded me, I would drink until it came.

For over a year I drank to the detriment of my physical health, social relationships and financial wellbeing, and it impacted my career severely. My colleagues and peers would surpass me in the workplace and be offered sought-after deployments and promotions, whilst I became bitter and resentful. I began to blame the institution for the fates that were befalling me. The disquiet in my mind stirred up by the abuse my stepfather subjected me to was what I now sought to suppress with alcohol. I was in the fledgling stages of alcoholism, and instead of being able to identify the correct cause of my self-destructive actions, I blamed my employer. Despite all the evidence that the Army had been good to me: employed me, given me a place to stay, granted me some of the best friends I would ever have and shown me parts of the world I would otherwise never have seen, I blamed it now for the anguish I was feeling. I convinced myself that the Army had done some great wrong to me and was the cause of all my problems. And so it – the faceless military organisation that paid my salary – would become the object of my loathing.

Even though my peers were excelling, attrition rates remained high within the company. Members of my basic training intake were soon amongst my company's most senior members despite only short military careers. This meant we were all highly sought after, irrespective of our mental disposition. And so, a time came when I was called away on exercise again, this time for six weeks, floating around the coastline of Australia on a naval vessel.

I haven't yet mentioned that I suffer feverishly from motion sickness, which is massively amplified at sea. So much so that I rely upon strong anti-nausea medicine, which essentially knocks me out, to see me through any kind of voyage. I used that medication during this exercise. Fortunately for me, my skill set was only required at three points during this exercise: at the start, the middle and the end. I spent the rest of those six weeks in an anti-nausea-induced coma. I was a complete and utter waste of space during that exercise, but no matter my outlook on life or the opinion of my employer, nothing could change the way my central nervous system receives messages from the sensory systems within my inner ear, requiring chemical intervention. Because of this I didn't touch booze for the duration of the entire exercise, but, thanks to the aforementioned coma, I was also granted reprieve from the demons I combated by drinking.

At the end of this exercise, due to my motion sickness, I was offered the option to fly instead of sail back to New Zealand, which I gratefully accepted – from Australia into Auckland, and then onto Palmerston North. I was anticipating drinking on the flight home, but refrained. It may have been the medication, or that I hadn't drunk in so long that the draw wasn't so strong, or perhaps there was no reason – but when the refreshments cart came around the aisles of the plane offering beer and wine, I declined both. Once the plane landed in Auckland I had some time to kill before transiting onto my next flight. There's not a lot to do in airports sans attending the bar; as I sat down I was feeling the pull to drink, not so much out of a chemical dependency or urge to silence the echo chamber in my brain, but out of habit and sheer boredom.

Whilst I was weighing up my options, I heard a familiar voice call my name – it was my Mum. "Alex!" she called out. I was surprised to see her, so said little before she explained her presence. She had been attending a conference for work in Auckland. It was nice to see her, I told her, and she reciprocated the kind words. Then she told me that there was news to share. We were standing in a crowded domestic departure lounge as my Mum informed me that my Uncle Anthony had passed away. I was utterly devastated; all I could manage to blurt out was, "When?" I was no longer at sea, but I felt dizzier now than I had done on that ship. My Mum told me that he had passed away in his sleep whilst visiting friends two weeks ago, and that the funeral had been held a few days back. I remember wishing I'd drained that refreshment cart of booze. Mum excused herself soon after – she was sorry and had to leave to catch her flight. I continued my travel back home to Palmerston North in a state of disbelief.

Upon returning to Linton I had a few days off, as was customary after any exercise or deployment. I did not drink nor leave my room, except for necessities. All I did was contemplate the news my Mum had given me. My Uncle Anthony had died, the man for whom I had so much love and admiration, yet whom I hadn't thought about in so long. I was griefstricken that I had been given the news so late, I was distraught about not being able to properly say goodbye to him, but I slowly began to accept the fact that he was gone. I remembered waving to him as I walked through the security gates the day I left for New Zealand. I reminisced over his involvement in my childhood and reflected on how he might view me now. I was certain he would not approve of my attachment to alcohol. I felt ashamed for the actions I had taken that lead me to become so dependent on alcohol. I knew that Anthony had always worked hard and dedicated himself to his task. He did this so that he could provide for the people he loved, including me. He did not misuse his time dwelling on past wrongs or seeking any kind of escape from reality; he got on with life with a focused and positive attitude. Thinking about what Anthony would have said about my life now was a powerful motivator to make some adjustments to it. Nothing was immediate, but with the help of the memories Anthony had left me from my childhood I started making some much needed, positive changes.

CHAPTER THIRTEEN

Reprieve, Repose

GETTING THAT BOOZE-SOAKED monkey off my back
was hard; but I did it, and it was in no small part thanks to
my Uncle Anthony's influence. Even though he was no longer around he still had a positive impact on my life, strong
enough to see me recover from an addiction to alcohol. I had
the benefit of a six-week head start thanks to the anti-nausea
medication I had taken, but it wasn't all smooth sailing from
there. There may have been a chemical component to my addiction, but it paled in comparison with the lure of escapism
that drinking offered me, much as my online gaming had provided in earlier years. Drinking offered me an opportunity to
rest from the suffering inside; but I had to break that habit.

Anyone who has tried to give up smoking, a very household addiction, will tell you that the habitual cues are some
of the hardest to shake and can linger long after the chemical
dependency has passed. I am not here to preach some kind
of proven rehabilitation method for alcoholics, I am just
telling my story. If you are struggling and you're big enough
to admit and acknowledge your issue, then I applaud you.
I hope you can get the help you need. I didn't reach out for
that help, and that was stupid. I just got lucky.

The first couple of weeks trying to break the cycle of drinking was a struggle. I didn't know what I was doing, I just knew my aim was not to drink. I booked myself two weeks' annual leave at short notice, and set about my task. I did nothing taxing or profound, I just tried to occupy myself. I watched movies, read books and played video games. I did it all from the confines of my room; whilst the guys in my barracks were by no means party animals, there was always the risk of walking in on a party around Linton, and I didn't want to risk the temptation. By the time my two weeks' hiatus was up I felt like I had broken the cycle – no booze had passed my lips, and I had a purpose for keeping it that way: I didn't want to be an embarrassment to Anthony's memory. I started hanging out with friends, playing console games and just having a laugh in the evenings, instead of drinking alone. I had a lot more money now that I wasn't drinking, so I started to buy nicer clothes and books, and took up reading. I also started exercising in my spare time. Since the Military mandated exercise during the day, I had given up doing it in my own time. Now I started going to the gyms in the evening, and taught myself how to properly lift weights.

Before long I was feeling great. You will notice the recurring theme: as I find new direction and purpose in my life, my perception of its quality improves; and in the absence of those things that perception rapidly deteriorates. The temptation to drink was still there, but as long as I distanced myself from the influence and distracted myself, I was fine. I had reconnected with my friends, some of whom I still consider to be amongst my closest. I found an interest in reading again and picked up a new hobby in weightlifting. The trajectory of my life had shot upwards in a steep arc. I felt better than before I started to drink, and I was no longer being tormented in my quiet moments alone. As my life became disciplined and routine-based again, my tormentors were driven back into their cage. The task of bettering myself to honour Anthony gave me the strength to lock the demons away. But whilst I felt better, I had not been freed. I was ignorant enough to believe I could be cured without addressing any of my past – a past I had not yet accepted.

The steady upward trajectory continued, spilling over from my personal life into my work. I began to perform better, and this was noticed by my superiors, who soon afforded me further development opportunities. Training in the Military was standard, everyone got it – but over the past year I had been offered the minimum, which was hardly surprising given the animosity I displayed towards the organisation that employed me and the superiors I believed represented it.

For the first time in a long while, maybe since before the abuse, I began to feel true self-worth. I was twenty-one years old at this point, and for the first time in recent memory I didn't feel like a worthless piece of shit. I even began to feel like I might be worth someone else's time; I began to want love. Men my age would ridicule the concept and make fun of people looking for relationship; the idea of a one-night stand was far more appealing and less complicated. I had no interest in a fling, though; I wanted someone to love me, and I was ready to put myself out there. But the only place I knew to meet single women was at bars, and I had been actively avoiding them for good reason. I was afraid to go it alone and risk losing the sobriety I had worked to achieve. I was worried that the temptation to drink might be too strong in these situations and cost me everything I had worked for since hearing the news of Anthony's passing. Sobriety aside, I also lacked any ability to talk to women without the aid of alcohol. For the first time ever, I did something profound: I reached out to friends for help and support. Supported by and accountable to people I was invested in and cared about, I was able to navigate bars without fear of relapse. I drew confidence from knowing I had their support. They helped me feel as if I was in control.

I don't really believe in karma or spiritual causality, but the positive attitude changes I was experiencing were having a profound effect on my own sense of wellbeing. I actually felt happy. That happiness reverberated around me and soon, as if by some cosmic act of fate, I met a girl. The first night that we met, our surroundings, a night club in Palmerston North, were far too loud for us to be able to have a decent conversation; lucky for me, because I might have told her I loved her then and there. We shared little with each other that evening, but there was an attraction between us. She had glowing fair skin, blonde hair and striking blue eyes, like deep pools of tranquil water you could soak in for hours and a smile that enveloped you in a warm embrace when you saw it. Her name was Thea. She was a student at the local university, staying in student accommodation. We would spend many evenings together in her room. We would share takeaway meals and watch movies together, laugh at each other's jokes and share our dreams for the future. It was the perfect little romance. I couldn't have known it at the time, but this girl, with whom I was rapidly falling in love, would become my champion, my stalwart defender and my strongest advocate in times to come.

Soon Thea and I moved in together. We fought and argued like any people sharing space do, but we also loved passionately, respected each other, and were always willing to accept each other's flaws. We would always forgive ourselves and be patient as each of us tried to improve ourselves for the benefit of the other. Life was good, and by the time I turned twenty-two Thea and I had bought our first home together. We stayed living in that same area for a while longer. Thea finished her studies and began working locally. We adopted several pets of our own and began fostering others. Thea loved animals, and by extension so did I.

But it was not long before both Thea and I grew restless and bored with the life the Military forced us to lead. It had a way of invading your private life unlike many other jobs. I was being called away frequently at short notice to work in harsh conditions, doing work I had no love for apart from Thea for months at a time. I had tried to let go of the animosity I felt towards the Army; Thea had become very aware of it, and felt it was ugly. I felt that my resentment was justified, but I was unable to release it. The strain that being called away was putting on my relationship only exacerbated the contempt I felt. I would discomfort Thea by continuing to complain bitterly to her, projecting my suppressed feelings for my abuser onto my employer, making the Army the object of my discontent. It served that purpose well, a patsy to occupy my demons which had not revisited me since I stopped drinking. I didn't stop to question why I felt so much unprovoked disdain for my employer, I just accepted it as fact. It was easier; that way I didn't need to think about my abuse or the horror I had endured.

In the year 2015 we said goodbye to Palmerston North. I was finally going to be free of the chains that I foolishly believed the Military had bound me in. I had applied for a job in Wellington City; Thea and I were moving to the Kāpiti Coast, an hour from Wellington. On that long drive to and from work I started avidly consuming podcasts, and my interest in self-improvement peaked. On the Kāpiti Coast I would finally come face to face with the reality of my abuse.

CHAPTER FOURTEEN

No Way to Heal

IT'S BEEN A bit of a journey to get here, hasn't it? You have learnt an awful lot of very personal stuff about me since that opening chapter in which I talked about wanting to drive into oncoming traffic. We're almost back at that point too. I'd forgive you for wondering how I managed to get myself from the relative high point in the last chapter to the absolute depths where this story began. To be completely truthful, I don't know the exact catalyst for the events that came before I dialled that number and made an appointment to see a counsellor, but I can tell you what I think.

I think of repressed memories like a cyst. Between freeing myself of alcohol-fuelled dependency on escapism and the later months of 2016, my abuse had absolutely zero airtime in my head. It was as if it had never happened. I still considered the Army the object of my loathing, I still continued a routine-based and disciplined approach to life, but most importantly, I had an amazing relationship with Thea. It was Sophocles who wrote, "One word frees us of all the weight and pain of life: that word is love". I believe there to be truth in that; from the moment we met I was in love with

Thea, and whether we were fighting or enjoying each other's company I was happiest when I was with her. We had actually gotten engaged and were to be married in December the following year; I couldn't wait.

I enjoyed the job I had moved to Wellington to take; it was very challenging and stressful, but also rewarding. The salary it offered was significantly better than my pay in the Army, which allowed Thea and I a better life than we ever would have had in the Military. Unfortunately it involved working some erratic shifts that disrupted the time I could spend with Thea, and made a regular sleep schedule seem like a pipe dream. I kept a routine of exercise and general activity, but neglected to adopt the same approach to rest. I believe many different stressors catalysed the rupture in the thin membrane of that repressed memory cyst; but being denied both time with the one person who brought me joy and one of the most basic requirements for survival, sleep, were definitely two of them. Whatever the root cause, soon that repressed cyst would tear, causing all of the vile memories and thoughts that lurked inside to erupt.

As you know, I dialled that number to arrange an appointment to see a counsellor; I followed through with it, too. There were no open slots for a few days following the phone call I made from my car; I would need to wait. I wasn't asked if I was suicidal, and I didn't tell them I was. The time between hanging up that phone and actually attending was plagued by the same voices with an added level of anxiety and self-hatred: "What have you even go to talk to them about, anyway? You're a waste of space, scum!" – and so they went on in my head. I had no desire to spill my guts to a stranger, but I would do it for Thea. Her support was enough to see me into the counsellor's office days later.

I had the address of the office I would need to find for my counselling. I didn't recognise the exact location, but I knew roughly where it was. Fortunately, as the appointment was mid-morning, I missed rush hour traffic. Without consciously deciding not to seek help I had been stalling talking to anyone for years now – a hold-up or obstacle at this stage might have been sufficient excuse for me to talk myself out of it. I drove back along the coastal road where I had been subjected to the barrage of abuse from the malevolence that lurked in my mind. On this journey I would have only silence and the hum of road noise to accompany me. As if to spite me, to make me second-guess the issues I had been experiencing, there was no sinister monologue on this journey; only dead air and road noise.

After parking my car the counsellor's office was only a short walk, according to the GPS on my phone. I pulled up my hood and put headphones in as I made my way down the street. It seems ridiculous, someone in my position being ashamed of seeking help, but I was. I didn't want anyone seeing me – they might guess where I was going, or worse, work out my secret! A ludicrous notion, but it caused me angst all the same. I mulled over some thoughts in my head as I put one foot in front of another – "Does this make me weak?" I worried. I had listened to podcasts and read books on being self-sufficient. As a subscriber to Stoic philosophy I had been taught through my reading that happiness should come from within. Marcus Aurelius wrote, "The happiness of your life depends upon the quality of your thoughts:

therefore, guard accordingly, and take care that you entertain no notions unsuitable to virtue and reasonable nature." So was I contradicting my beliefs by reaching out for help? At that moment, thinking that I may be dishonouring the great man by possibly contradicting his teachings almost saw me turn around and go home. At the time I would have benefited from reminding myself that Marcus Aurelius also wrote, "Don't be ashamed of needing help. You have a duty to fulfill just like a soldier on the wall of battle. So what if you are injured and can't climb up without another soldier's help?" He literally teaches us that it is ok to seek help.

My irrational fears and worries kept me bound up in a tight cocoon of anxiety all the way to my destination. Looming before me was a dreary, weather-beaten office building which housed the counselling service I was to visit. I stepped inside the lobby which was poorly lit and cold, to observe a coffee shop that was closed. Adjacent to that was a shopfront that appeared to have belonged to a barber at one time or another, but now was simply a ghoulish husk of its former self. I stood in that lobby, taking in my surroundings, feeling isolated and afraid. The elevators I would need to ride were at the end of the lobby; I approached them and pushed the call button. Before entering I turned and looked back out to the street at the people walking by. I felt confident none of them would be entering this eerily dystopian office block, it wasn't the type of place out of which any kind of profitable industry would operate; this helped to calm my nerves – I didn't want to be seen. I wondered how those people, going about their lives unaware of my observations, would judge me if they were to learn the purpose for my presence in that lobby. In that moment I didn't actively consider the stigma that surrounds talking about mental health, but I felt its presence more than ever that morning. I stepped into the elevator; there was a damp smell. I selected the floor I needed on the panel, a light blinked through the dirt and grime that had congealed over it. My mind began to race again, standing in that claustrophobic elevator: "I don't need to be here, this was a mistake, a waste of time. It's a free service, perhaps I'll just ..." – a familiar ding rang out, and the doors creaked open, interrupting my train of thought.

I was distracted by my surroundings as I stepped out. I stood in a small, claustrophobic corridor painted bleach white, with a foggy glass door at one end. Two chairs were positioned just in front of where I had exited the elevator, separated by a small table with various leaflets arranged on it, all depicting people smiling. There was no sign of life here, and I began to wonder if I was in the right place. This wasn't the stereotypical therapist's office that TV had prepared me for. Where were the leather couches, oak bookshelves holding leather-bound books and tweed-clad, thick-rimmed-spectacle-wearing therapists? Not here. To be honest, I'm not certain what I expected to find upon stepping out of the elevator, but it certainly wasn't this soulless corridor, devoid of life. The sheer jarring contrast between the dystopian lobby and this clinical, soulless holding area were enough to induce a panic attack. I found myself wanting to back into the lift, and I was looking for any excuse when the door at the end of the corridor clicked, like a latch being lifted. I stared as a lady's face appeared around the door. "Alex?" she asked. "Yes," was my response. "This way please," she beckoned, now fully emerging through the door and holding it open for me.

The lady who greeted me was small in stature, I noted, as I walked into another desolate corridor through which I was quickly ushered by my vertically challenged concierge, and into an office where she shut the door behind her. Taking a seat at a small desk in the corner of the office, she gestured for me to sit down. There was only one other seat in the room, with a small plastic body and a metal frame like you can find in many schools. It was positioned immediately opposite her, uncomfortably close. This office matched everything else I have seen here, barren but not as bleached white: slightly more yellowy brown, almost dirty, like someone used to smoke in here regularly. Barely a sentence had been uttered at this point, yet it felt as if I had been here for ever. Everything so far has been discomforting, including the audible tapping now happening on the keyboard in front of me. The cocoon of anxiety I was wrapped in had morphed into a sarcophagus full of spikes closing in on me. I had promised Thea I would talk to someone about what was going on – I was not about to go back on what I said, but everything about this place was making it hard to keep my word.

The lady, who by now I had decided must be my therapist, swivelled in her chair to face me. She was middle-aged with dark hair, wearing grey and brown clothes; there was nothing alarming about her appearance. Despite what felt like a cold reception, she seemed friendly. Looking me in the eye she smiled, and then asked me that dreaded question: "So, what's brought you here today?" I'm unsure if at that point the temperature in the room jumped twenty degrees, or if that was just my perception – but I felt hot, and my chest felt as if some disgusting ogre was trying to crush it. I diverted my eyes away from her gaze and started fidgeting with my hands. I wanted to make a snide comment suggesting I'd got here in the elevator, or that working out why I was here was her job, but I refrained. I felt angry and upset, but that wasn't her fault. I coughed as if to clear my throat, and croaked, "I've just been feeling a little down, lately", whilst really giving my shoes a good examination.

I'm not here to criticise anyone working in the mental health sector, but I felt as if I was giving off all kinds of warning signs that I was hiding something or had more to say. Despite all these signs, what came after my admission of feeling a little down was possibly the most boring ten minutes of my life. We discussed deep breathing, counting to ten and understanding other people's perspectives in the workplace. I was given an unreasonable number of pamphlets regarding said techniques. I wanted to get up and leave, I wanted to scream out of frustration; but by the end of the educational chat I was simply bored. Then it dawned on me – this was a *workplace* counselling service. Of course they would be talking to me about workplace issues! It wasn't fair of me to expect anything else. At the cessation of our enlightening chat, the kindly counsellor locked eyes with me again and smiled: "Is there anything else you'd like to discuss?" I pondered that question for a moment. I was adamant in my mind that there wasn't, yet I still hadn't kept my word to Thea – I had told her I would talk to someone. "Yes," I uttered. "No!" mocked my subconscious. All of the sensations I felt at her initial question came on again, the ogre's fist clamped around my chest again – I wouldn't be able to talk even if I tried. I imagined myself saying the words, but could do nothing else. I became increasingly aware of my surroundings and the four walls enveloping me like they were leaning in, making the space smaller. The spikes from my sarcophagus were closing once more as I winced and began to relive my journey into this office. The dystopian lobby, unnervingly scented elevator and padded cell-esque corridors – but faster this time, like I was sprinting through time. I felt unwell.

Then something odd happened: those words I was imagining started coming out of my mouth. I felt like I wasn't in control, I was an observer once more. I watched myself tell her everything from somewhere else in the room. "I was sexually abused by my stepfather." I listened as I told her everything in graphic detail – and not just about Ernest and how he had abused me, but the lack of connection I felt with my family, my grief at not being able to see my father. I divulged how Ernest began visiting me when we lived in Sandhurst, the unrest I felt at moving all the time. The floodgates had opened, and it was all spilling out. I told her how Ernest first penetrated me in Spain and how his abuse escalated to frequent rape from then on, my escaping into the world of games and disconnecting from reality. I admitted to manipulating people and worming my way into their lives so I could feel a sense of belonging at their expense, the decision to move to New Zealand, struggling with alcohol, the grief and lack of closure with Anthony's death, how I felt dishonest with Thea and most recently an overwhelming desire to die. Perhaps it had been the security that I felt with the perceived anonymity of counselling that caused this flurry of honesty, or perhaps my state of panic triggered my acute stress response to step in and save me once again. There had been a subconscious, intrinsic pressure from the years of repression that just had to be released. Once I had finished, I felt myself float back into my body and I felt good, momentarily.

The counsellor looked at me; I could see her processing all that I had said. She looked tense and I saw her eyes looking in my direction, darting around, but not at me. I had made her uncomfortable. Seconds passed, and I began to panic again. Now there were two of us in the world that knew my secrets. Shit. Still nothing was said. Then there was movement – my counsellor turned to her computer and she said something strange, along the lines that she wouldn't take any notes so that there would be no record of what I said. Now I was really panicked – did what I said here get fed back to my employer? Was that part of the fine print of them funding the service? Shit. The ogre was now doing its best to squeeze the life out of me, breathing was hard, the walls were leaning in further than ever. The counsellor told me she wouldn't book me another follow-up session, but perhaps I should book a doctor's appointment and get some medication. That I was clearly depressed.

I don't remember thanking her for her time, I don't remember what I did with the pile of leaflets she had given me, and I don't remember leaving that building. I remember being out on the street with my hood up again and headphones in my ears, feeling utterly ashamed, like there was no way for me to heal. My eyes were darting under my hood making sure no one was watching me, that no one had recognised me. I was walking at a quickened pace, the demons in my head gleefully harassing me over the sound of my music: "You stupid arse, there's nothing wrong with you, what have you done now? You can't undo what you did." The taunting was relentless – I felt as if I'd done something wrong, I felt worse than I did before. Everything felt abrasive and offensive, I was angry and upset. I made it back to my car and threw open the door before climbing in. I had hot tears in my eyes. I had failed. I'd told Thea I would talk to someone, and I couldn't even do *that* properly. Obviously I'd said something wrong to the counsellor, or she would have been kinder to me, helped me even. Instead I was told to go and get some medicine. Obviously there was something wrong with me. I felt broken.

Naturally, Thea wanted to talk about the events of the day when she got home from work that evening; she even had a sympathetic yet optimistic smile on her face as she asked me about it. How was I going to explain to her what had unfolded in the counsellor's office? Could I explain to her that the whole way home and up until the point she walked through the door I had been imagining ways to kill myself? No, I couldn't bring myself to do that to her.

Thea loved me and was genuinely concerned. Whatever was going on in my head I could have told her and not been judged; she would have been genuinely compassionate, understanding and supportive, I loved her for that. But I lied to her. I have my excuses and my reasons, but ultimately that's what it boils down to: I was dishonest. I wanted to tell her the truth, but I couldn't bear to. Since I'd left the counsellor I'd been chastising myself for talking; I felt that I should have just said nothing, just pulled my socks up and carried on. I was disgusted with myself for feeling how I did – I should just man up and deal with it. Numerous podcast hosts and social media icons had told me, indirectly whilst addressing global audiences, that I had the power within me, that I could do anything if I set my mind to it. So why couldn't I feel better? I must be a failure.

I couldn't just say nothing, though; I wanted to tell her everything. I wanted to be honest with the woman I loved. I started imagining the words just as I had in the counsellor's office. "I was sexually abused ..." I stuttered, observing Thea's eyes widening in disbelief, "... as a child" – I couldn't get anything else out. "By whom?" asked Thea. That's the point where I started lying. I fabricated some faceless phantom who was familiar with my family at the time of my childhood. He was such good friends with my family that he was able to gain access to me when I was vulnerable. That's what I told her. I offered no more details of the abuse I suffered.

Thea was shocked at my tale and wanted to know who it was. I replied that I didn't properly know them and that there was no chance of us ever meeting them again, that they were in no way associated with my family anymore. I thought about Ernest: Thea knew Ernest – what would happen if she ever found out he did those things to me? She knew him as he was now, as a quirky old man who seemed harmless to casual observers. I felt sick. All I had to do was say his name and tell her it was him; he was the Phantom. But I couldn't do it. My family's lives would be changed for ever if I did, ruined like mine was.

I wasn't ready to tell her the truth, so I volunteered more information from my counsellor's appointment in its place. I coloured the rest of my account with a far more positive lens to try and ease the situation, primarily for my own benefit. There was little reality in what I said, other than that she had advised me to get medication. Thea was shaken by the revelation that I may be depressed, but promised to support me however she could, told me she would always be there for me, and held me. Despite my dishonesty, I felt safe.

Medication had always been a touchy subject for me. I didn't want to be reliant on it for something I should be able to do myself. I had the notion in my mind that it was a form of weakness, which I know now to be completely incorrect. Fortunately, I had shared the counsellor's recommendation with Thea, who was adamant that I make an appointment with our doctor to follow through with a prescription. I went to work that day and when I got a quiet moment I called my doctor's practice to book in, I told the person who picked up the phone that I was making the appointment at the behest of a counsellor I had seen, due to feelings of depression and anxiety. The receptionist didn't ask me if I was suicidal, nor did I volunteer that information. I was booked in for 3pm; I waited in the waiting room until after 5pm to see my General Practitioner. When I left, I had a script for antidepressants.

Chapter Fifteen

Maslow

I AM STEPPING away from telling my story again for another short chapter. Retelling events is a difficult undertaking and it pays to change the subject for a while, for me at least.

Since finding closure I have often revisited and analysed the period in my life I described in the last chapter. Would things have been different for me if I had been brave enough to be honest with Thea in the first instance? Did talking with the counsellor help me? Why, at this time in my life when things were going so well for me, did I crash so low? Surely, if I was going to experience a deep and depressive state it would have made sense for that to develop when I had nothing, when I lived with Clare, had to move back to New Zealand to live with Ernest once more, or became dependent on alcohol to get through the days. Why did it come when I had a loving partner, my own house and a stable income? I can't say for sure, but since then I have read a thing or two about a man named Abraham Maslow. He theorised a concept called the Hierarchy of Needs. Whilst criticised and contested academically, this concept has helped me rationalise how I felt during that period.

Maslow theorised that human beings have five categories of needs, starting with basic physiological needs and advancing to more complex needs. The basic mechanic at play here is that once a need is fulfilled, the next "higher need" becomes the focus of our attention.

Before continuing, I would just like to make you aware of the Merriam-Webster definition of the word 'need', being "a physiological or psychosocial requirement for the well-being of an organism". In a world where we have taken words with a literal definition and applied colloquial, anecdotal meanings to them before dropping them into our everyday vernacular, I feel that it is important that we clarify how I intend for you to interpret the word before I ask you to accept it as a premise for a theory. I'm not suggesting for even a second that you don't know what the word 'need' means, but nowadays the word 'need' is becoming more and more commonly interchangeable with the word 'want', which has an entirely less severe definition. Now, where were we?

Abraham Maslow's work paved the way for the field that would become known as Positive Psychology, primarily because he sought to understand people instead of simply trying to diagnose a fault with them. The Positive Psychology movement, whilst excellent, is superfluous to what I want to talk about here, so I will step over that rabbit hole before I fall down it and share tea with the Mad Hatter.

So we have Maslow's Hierarchy of Needs, not to be confused with Asimov's Laws of Robotics, which is commonly visually represented in pyramid form. The most basic needs appear towards the bottom and the higher needs toward the top. Listed from bottom to top with some examples of what he meant in brackets, Maslow identified our needs as: Physiological (Food, Water, Shelter, Sleep), Safety Needs (Personal Security, Employment, Health, Property), Love and Belonging (Friendship, Intimacy, Family, Sense of Connection), Esteem (Respect, Self-Esteem, Status, Recognition, Strength, Freedom) and Self-Actualisation (Desire to be the best version of one's self). I am not going to ask you to accept Maslow's theories, simply that you humour me while I use it as a metric to rationalise why I was in such a state, because I have found it to be quite fitting and a helpful tool for understanding my thoughts.

Starting from the bottom, as is logical (unlike some people who start writing books in the middle of their story), I was capable of meeting all of my physiological needs with the exception of good sleep: this was frequently plagued by negative thoughts and sinister internal dialogue, both of which were particularly bad in the period of my life that we are currently examining. However, an imperfectly satisfied need does not necessarily prevent one from becoming focused on a more advanced need. If, for example, you present a man two options by which he may be fed – a healthy and nutritious salad, or a greasy cheeseburger – he will be nourished regardless of which option he chooses, thus allowing him to focus his attention elsewhere. Whilst my sleep was not of a good standard, I was rested and able to move on with my day.

The next tier of needs is where things get more complicated: Safety Needs. During the period of time discussed in the previous chapter, I should theoretically have had very few security concerns of any nature. I was young, physically fit, six foot three inches tall, a powerlifter (with a two-hun-dred-and-fifty-kilogram deadlift), and an ex-soldier with close-quarter battle training. At home Thea and I had good locks on the doors and windows, the house was on a qui-et street, it was equipped with a home security system, we had a large German Shepherd who was very territorial, our neighbours were friendly, and Thea was also an accom-plished martial artist. My job, which I enjoyed, paid well and was in demand both domestically and overseas. Thea was in a similar position with her work, and we had a buffer of sav-ings that we could live off for months, should either or both of us be made redundant. There were no obvious or likely risks to my health, personal or financial security or my em-ployment, yet I felt so insecure.

My perception of my own safety in all respects had been drastically skewed by the abuse I suffered at the hands of my stepfather. I had not been safe in my own bed as a child sur-rounded by family, so how could I feel safe anywhere? I felt extreme anxiety at even the slightest chance of conflict in any form. Whilst I am (and was then) intelligent, strong and capable of defending myself, I was scared that anyone would become annoyed with me, verbally berate me and leave me feeling embarrassed and belittled. Perhaps they would even become physically violent and overpower me at a moment's notice. There had been times when my acute stress response had responded to threats of violence against me, but I didn't control that. Ridiculous anxieties, but ones I felt legitimately and perpetually. Consequently I would steer clear of any sit-uation requiring me to be assertive, or with even the slightest chance of resulting in conflict. Thea wanted to purchase a larger house, yet I refused for the longest time as I was terrified of losing my job and becoming penniless. I knew my job and Thea's were secure; I could see the money in our bank account providing us stability; yet these facts did nothing to ease my fears. I was not capable of feeling at peace, as I felt like I meant nothing to anyone and had no understanding that people might value my opinions or presence. I had no sense of self-worth.

All sense of love and belonging had been taken from me and buried alive somewhere inside me. I struggled to maintain friendships for the same reasons I believed I wold be sacked at any moment: I felt as if I were worthless. I wouldn't reach out to talk to anyone – I would feel I was a drain on them. Most human relationships rely on a minimum of two basic factors: some common ground over which communication and a bond can be established, as well as continued effort to maintain that communication and bond. Because of my perception of myself, I would neither establish nor maintain such bonds often or actively. I loved Thea, and believed she loved me because of the things she told me, and the way she acted and behaved towards me. I would try to reciprocate these actions but would regularly fail. We survived as a couple because she was patient, she did not give up on me, and took the time to remind me that she loved me and, most importantly, why. Without her stalwart commitment to me and our life together, I don't think we would have made it; I know I wouldn't have. I am incredibly grateful to her and everything she did for me. At times I was definitely neglectful: compassion was not something that would occur to me, and I would seldom initiate the romantic gestures or activities which help a relationship thrive. Testament to how incredible she really is.

I had no sense of family; my family in New Zealand was tainted by Ernest's presence, and I had been cut off from my family in England, first by being forbidden to see them and then by the fact that they lived in a different hemisphere. I can acknowledge that I was trying to find a sense of connection in many things I did. Joining the Army, joining power-lifting teams and even online gaming were attempts at forming a sense of community and belonging, but I was never able to connect with them properly.

All avenues toward developing esteem were shut off to me. Respect, self-esteem, status, recognition, strength or freedom – all were closed. My self-image was no different than when I was a young boy being molested by an older man and powerless to stop it. That's all I saw myself as. In reality I was a successful, strong, intelligent young man with an apparently great life that could have been the envy of others – but all of that was for naught, rendered void by my perception of myself. When I looked in the mirror, I saw a coward. A coward who, instead of standing up for himself when his oppressor would visit, pretended to be asleep as he climbed all over him, allowing him to do whatever he wanted as he took pictures to share with his perverted friends on the internet. As a result, I actively rejected status or recognition; I would even dodge having photographs taken whenever I could. I didn't want to be seen. When your own thoughts are tainted, you can't escape or hope to change them – they are you, and you can't escape yourself. You can only hope to accept; but even that is a challenge without help.

Now we reach the pinnacle of the pyramid, the last item on Maslow's Hierarchy of Needs: Self-Actualisation. At this time I was knee deep in 'self-improvement', attempting to actualise myself. Whilst I was unhappy and aware that everything was not fine, I wasn't allocating blame properly, or associating my abuse with how I felt. I thought I must be missing something, lacking some skill or piece of knowledge that was holding me back. I threw myself headfirst into the wormhole of books with titles like "Biohacking your mind for success", "30 days to this or that", "X things that you are missing that are holding you back", the majority of which were terrible books in their own right but also served to further convince me that I needed more work, to buy the author's next book or attend their seminars that could be streamed for a small fee in order to move past my (apparently) obvious limitations. Social media is rampant with this stuff. I listened to podcasts featuring life coaches and experts who knew exactly what I needed to do in order to fix my non-specific predicament. Social media only served to further my worry: constantly being bombarded with images of successful people who were definitely living their best lives and couldn't wait to tell you how hard they worked to garner all the fame and success they had now and sell you their ideas on how you can achieve their status too. It was all bullshit, but in the state I was in, I bought it. Believing I was lacking something was easier than accepting my past and acknowledging the memories I was trying to ignore.

There was no way that I would be able to meet my basic needs before accepting what I had been subjected to as a boy. To do that I would have to learn to properly allocate blame, to realise it wasn't my fault. That wouldn't come for a while yet. Instead I dived deeper still into the dark ocean of Self-Improvement. Articles would give me the idea that my diet wasn't dialled-in enough – I still ate things I liked from time to time. Soon food became fuel; if it wasn't optimal, I didn't want it. Someone else out in the vast expanse of the internet was blowing her own trumpet about how reading so many books a month made her a better person; I didn't have that kind of time, but I wasn't going to risk missing that crucial piece of the puzzle. As a result I stopped listening to music during workouts, and instead had audiobooks playing throughout. Not entertaining books, either – books in the same vein that got me here, telling me what I was insufficient in, how and where I needed to improve. Each new book identified a new area that I was failing in. I turned to my workouts – perhaps they were not delivering the results they should. Soon I found myself training in three different disciplines for up to three hours some days just so I wasn't missing anything. This was not a healthy frame of mind to be in, and I was exhausted as a result, but also ashamed of myself for not being able to identify that crucial skill I clearly did not possess. I did not share my activities with anyone, I didn't discuss my triumphs or achievements, topics I found curious or things I simply didn't understand; I just kept it all bottled up. As a result my moods worsened, pushing me further down inside myself until it was pitch black. I used to try and escape my reality through gaming and drinking; now I was simply trying to cover it all up by attaching my self-worth to the obsessive pursuit of self-improvement. My prospects were bleak, but things had to get bad for Thea to put the pressure on me to get help. Even though my first attempt was unsuccessful it was a start, and did eventually lead to the truth coming out so that I could start my recovery. Like the old saying goes, "It's always darkest before the dawn."

So, why did I begin to feel so rotten at *this* time in my life, rather than when things were already going badly for me? Surely if there was a time to be depressed it was back when I was out of shape, eating like shit, seldom sleeping, boozing every night, working a shit job and living with a girl I knew I had manipulated into liking me. Looking through Maslow's lens, it's a little clearer why. When I was living with Clare and even when I was in the Army, I was either unable to fulfil or was completely neglecting my basic needs. By denying myself those needs on the bottom rung of the hierarchy, higher needs could never hold the focus of my attention, meaning that I would never be distressed by my inability to fulfil them. Even when I had met Thea and we bought our first house together, just servicing our basic needs was a struggle because of financial pressures.

I am not a trained expert, and you may not accept my premise. But that is my own explanation for my feelings. I see it as the curse of contradiction with which Ernest hexed me. As a result of my abuse I was doomed to feel worse and worse as life got better. I should have felt amazing and been happy during the previous chapter, free to live without all that darkness welling up inside me. But because of him I was cursed to feel awful, and there was no way out of it, only through it.

Chapter Sixteen

Chemical Alleviation

I LEFT THE doctor's that day with a prescription for antidepressants, and I started the course. Reluctantly at first – but then they started making me feel better. Soon I was returning to the doctor to up the dosage, and there I would stay, pleasantly numb of my pain for months. The pills allowed me to ignore everything I felt the next time I saw Ernest; like water off a duck's back, those feelings just slid away. My pus-filled cyst of repressed memories had burst and I knew who he was now, yet I was able to look at him as just a quirky pervert who bumbled around the place and nothing more, thanks to the soft blanket of chemicals in which the medication had ensconced my brain. I mistook this comfortable inertia for happiness, fooling myself into thinking that this whole time I just needed medicating and that for the rest of my life all I had to do to keep being happy was to go down to the pharmacy and fill a prescription. That's not living. We are all a sum of our struggles and our pain; they make up a lot of what defines us as people. I allowed the pills to strip all that away.

I am not anti-medication, not at all. I don't like taking pills, but that's not because of the misguided belief I once held about them making you dependent or weak – I just don't like the feeling as they go down your throat. But I support medication, and believe it to be important – just not in the way that I used them. I relied on them to block my emotions, so I didn't have to feel anything. I was denying my memories of what Ernest had done, despite knowing deep down what he was and what he had done to me. I knew he was to blame, but I was all fucked up inside and couldn't acknowledge it. The antidepressants took away the conflict that existed because of that. I should have attended therapy at the same time, but I was complacent and ignorant. I let myself believe the pills had fixed me. Instead they threw a rug over a stain, a tarpaulin over a broken window, a bucket under a leak. If you do what I did, be warned; eventually whatever you are trying to soak up or hide will seep through again.

I was still myself whilst on medication, however high the dose was. I wasn't whisked away to some magical fairy land where traffic jams are rainbows and cancer is just another name for a holiday in the Caribbean; I still occupied the same space and mind, but my emotional pain was hidden from me. I still obsessed over self-improvement and would beat myself up over skills I was lacking, but to a lesser degree now. Time still passed in the same fashion as it always had done. As I mentioned earlier, Thea and I were engaged to be married. A year or so had passed between that horrendous counselling session, and now Thea and I had moved house (the story of Thea convincing me to do that is a book in itself – the medication likely helped) and I had taken a less stressful job with more reasonable hours – I just couldn't keep doing what I had been. Soon our wedding day arrived. It was wonderful, and I will never forget it. It's one of my happiest memories, right next to welcoming my daughter into the world. All of my happiest memories have been with Thea right by my side and I by hers. On that day we swore to love each other and support each other in kind. We read vows; words written out of true love, for better or for worse. Thea would not foresee the worse coming so soon. We made speeches, danced and celebrated with our loved ones. Yet even that wonderful day was tarnished by the fact that Ernest was there. At the time the pills made me completely impartial to his presence, as if he was just one of the crowd – the medication worked wonders. But I will regret not acting sooner for the rest of my life. Yet another time that disease of a man was able to infect my life, and yet another time that I allowed it to happen.

Like most heteronormative couples, once married, Thea and I wanted to start a family together. We were both so excited to share this decision. We told Thea's family first; they were over the moon at the concept, as were our friends. Everyone we met knew we were in love, and with my abuse completely buried under a good pile of chemically induced dirt nothing appeared to be casting a shadow over us. Until the day we told my Mum and Ernest of our decision.

We met on a Saturday in the Wairarapa, a region famous for its wine, at a winery restaurant looking out onto a picturesque vineyard with green rolling hills as a backdrop. We all shared small talk over lunch until Thea and I decided we had stalled long enough, and told them our news with an excited shyness. My Mum reacted with an exclamation of joy followed by a hug, telling us it was great news. Ernest grinned and nodded; I can't remember his words. I just remember looking at him. A multitude of masked feelings must have been evoked within me; I felt uneasy from that moment on until much later in the day, but I was able to hide my discomfort for a short while. I had just told the man who had raped me when I was young and abused me for years that I planned to have children of my own; he was happy about it. Those little pills I had been gleefully popping for months now hid from me whatever feelings were trying to boil over.

We returned home that evening, but I was unable to reconcile the dissonance and discomfort I felt. I began to feel dark – dark and heavy is the only way I can describe it, like there was some kind of star collapsing inside my head. I stopped wanting to talk, eat, sleep or do anything. I didn't have suicidal thoughts, I just felt what I can only describe as an utter dread, like death itself had its gaze upon me. This went on for weeks after our rendezvous. Weeks, until Thea put her foot down and told me it was time to go and talk to someone again. She did not lose her temper with me or demand I "pull my socks up", or take any number of available, unhelpful stances. She recognised something was wrong and that I needed help, but also that she wouldn't be equipped to help me. I dodged the issue for many days before agreeing with her. I wasn't sure who I was going to talk to, but I knew one thing: it would not be the same people I saw last time.

I lack the necessary vocabulary to properly describe the state I slipped into; the most accurate description I can conjure is that of a trance. I was aware of what was happening around me but felt no concern for it. Hunger, thirst, fatigue and boredom all seemed superfluous now – nothing mattered. I just watched the world go by in front of my eyes as I slipped in and out of this trance involuntarily. In one lucid period I decided I would talk to my doctor about counselling. During my visits throughout the year he had not probed any further into why I continued on the medication he was prescribing me; but he had always come across as understanding and compassionate. I was certain that a confidentiality agreement exists between a doctor and their patient, so I felt alright about talking to him. In New Zealand there is limited funding for public health care, meaning if you want to see a medical professional outside of emergencies you need to pay, and it isn't cheap. I hoped my doctor knew a good counsellor, or this would be a very expensive and awkward waste of time.

As it happened, I was in luck – there was a counselling service run out of the same building, with several appointments funded through one scheme or another. As with my previous counselling roughly twelve months prior, there was a wait, a week this time. I was not asked if I was suicidal, but I did volunteer the information that I had been not so long ago; I was given a leaflet to read because of this admission.

Another week passed. I continued to take my medication when I remembered, and involuntarily drifted in and out of that trance-like state, listening to people getting frustrated with me at work and other places while remaining completely unfazed. I didn't have control. As to the exact thoughts that ran through my mind in this state, I can offer you nothing further. I can only be certain of one thing, and that is that time passed and eventually my appointment came.

Patrick was the counsellor I spoke with that day. I did not have to traverse a dystopian wasteland to reach him. I turned up to the doctor's office, and the nurse called my name to come forward when the time came for my appointment. I felt like everybody else in the room. I was shown to an office in the same hallway I would usually traverse to visit my doctor, the only difference being that this time it was a different person waiting for me. Nobody there would have any reason to believe this was anything other than a regular GP visit.

Patrick greeted me warmly as I entered the room. He was a friendly man of German descent, he enjoyed music and socialising, and lived with his wife – not locally, but also not too far away. I learnt these things about Patrick, including his name, within minutes of meeting him. I was not as forthcoming, but he managed to pry a lot of information from me without coming across as intrusive. I had just met the man, but he validated my presence, made me feel welcome, and became invested in my life beyond the issue I was presenting with. He treated me like a human being, not a problem that needed investigating and addressing. As we talked for a few more minutes, I began to feel a lot more relaxed around this man I was already getting to know. He then asked me if I would like to discuss the reason for booking the appointment to see him. I told him I would. Patrick then told me I could take as long as I wanted and to let him know when I was ready. At this point he had no idea what I was going through or my background, but he had shown me nothing but respect and genuine interest, and he was willing to extend as much of his patience as was required for me to comfortably discuss the reason for my presence in a counsellor's office. I felt like I could trust him, and whilst I still felt uneasy in myself, I was comfortable telling him everything from start to finish. I spoke for a long time whilst Patrick listened, made notes, and offered me assurance when I was finding it hard to keep going. I finished recounting my experiences, and Patrick actually thanked me for sharing my tale.

Soon after I'd finished, Patrick helped me figure out what I wanted to do next, without putting words in my mouth or confusing me. Between us we decided that all I wanted to do in the first instance was tell Thea. He then asked me about her, our story, how we met, and our ambitions. He got to know Thea through me and once he felt he did, he told me that everything would be ok, and I could feel safe telling her. I already knew that, but for some reason Patrick's assurance made me more confident in my belief. He told me that if I wanted to, I could call him to discuss it further before I spoke with Thea. As our session was ending he told me he would like me to come back and see him very soon – he even encouraged me to bring Thea along. That was the end of my session, but not the last time I would see Patrick. I went to him a complete and utter wreck and I left still a bit of a mess, but significantly more secure in my next course of action.

Patrick by no means fixed me – but he validated my feelings, made me feel valued and trusted, whilst assuring me I could reach out to my loved ones. I will be forever grateful for how he helped me that day. I wish that everyone looking for help could find a Patrick. If he had been waiting for me at the top of that soulless office building a year previously, perhaps I would have been spared the shame of having Ernest at my wedding, and could have protected Thea and my family from him that much sooner. Such thoughts are no good to me now, though.

I returned home after seeing Patrick and I knew what I was going to do next – I was going to be honest with Thea. I have faced many physically hard challenges in my life: I completed basic training for the Army, ran a marathon in Antarctica, then again in Dubai, and have lifted what many would consider backbreaking weights. Nor have the adversities I've overcome been limited to physical feats: I endured sexual abuse and rape for years, dealt with anxiety and depression, overcame addiction in different forms, educated myself so that I could build a life beyond what I probably should have been capable of, and I have endeavoured to be the best man that I can be for Thea. None of these things were as hard as being truthful with Thea that day.

It was something that mystified me for a while. Thea, since I have known her, has been the person I trust the most, the one who brings me joy in life. I share everything with her and would happily trust her with my life; yet I was unable to tell her about my abuse and about the man my stepfather really was. I know the reason why now, and it is because that meant being honest with myself. If I told Thea the truth, then everything I had bottled up inside since the repressed memories burst from that cyst would become reality again. Everything I denied, hid and suppressed would be released into the world. Not only would she know who my stepfather was, but *I* would have to accept it as well. I would have to be truthful with myself, pills or no pills. I would have to come to terms with the fact that every decision I made had unintentionally protected him and kept him protected. Somehow, I would have to accept that I had allowed a paedophile who had raped me and photographed me afterward continue to live a life in society, possibly harming others in the same way he had hurt me – and I would have to live with myself afterwards.

That evening, I told Thea everything. That I had lied to her, that the phantom molester had in fact been Ernest. I told her what he had done to me, how I kept it secret, and the effect that had had on me. I told her I was sorry. Do I need to tell you of the contempt she had toward Ernest? The phrase "hell hath no fury" applied well. That evening I shared my pain with the person I love. I listened to her anger, grief, shock and disdain. We tried to fathom the impact the fall-out from this news would have on the rest of my family. We talked honestly about my abuse for the first time, and I felt the weight on my shoulders lift just a little. It was the hardest thing I have ever done, but out of that challenge I gained my most fierce champion, my stalwart protector – and we would have retribution.

I think anyone who has loved someone who has been hurt will sympathise with Thea here; she wanted to get in the car that night and go deal to Ernest. If events had happened in a different order I might have agreed with her and, once again, have been writing this book under different circumstances. This was the first time I had been honest with myself about my abuse. I had no choice now but to begin accepting it; I was still not ok with it, but now I had brought Thea into my story of abuse it became more real. It had always been real, but locked away in a compartment of the past in my mind, for the most part. Now it was part of the present and required action. After cooling off just a little, Thea sprang into action; she picked up the phone and began to search for services that could help me further.

CHAPTER SEVENTEEN

Kintsugi

AT FIRST THEA'S attempts at finding me more assistance met with moderate to severe frustration. She took a far more structured approach than I had ever managed, calling various rape hotlines and mental health support services looking to be directed to a specific organisation that could assist me with my issues. Initially her attempts turned up nothing – all of the crisis and help lines were either specifically for women who had experienced rape, or only concerned with suicide prevention. No one knew where to direct a mid-twenties male who was finally coming to terms with his childhood trauma of rape and sexual abuse. If it had been me, I would have likely given up looking at that point and gone about trying to tackle things my own way and probably ended up back at square again, or worse – but Thea did not falter.

Admitting something has happened to you is hard, but a step in the right direction. *Accepting* something has happened, whilst it may seem somewhat trivial after admitting it, is harder but just as necessary. After admitting to myself that I was a sexual abuse survivor, I could have just got on with my life, maybe tried to forgive Ernest for what he did to me and moved on. *Accepting* that I was a sexual abuse survivor and slotting that chapter of my life into my timeline – allowing it to shape who I am and truly recovering from the effects the abuse had wrought upon me – required more work. I wanted to do that work; I wanted closure and justice, I wanted to see that he did not hurt anyone else. But I needed help. Thea knew that and supported me, which is why she was so resourceful and committed in her efforts.

Eventually Thea had a call back and was directed to an organisation called Mosaic, specifically established to assist male survivors of sexual abuse. Once I reached out to them, they were prepared to see me as soon as I could make it in.

Mosaic is an excellent organisation doing work in an area that is currently lacking a voice. No form of sexual abuse towards anyone is acceptable, but it does happen to so many people, including men. It happens to men when they are younger, and when they are older. I was subjected to a form of grooming as a child, as my stepfather normalised his presence in my room after dark. He sexually abused me as a teenager and went on to rape me. He may even have done other things during that time that I can't remember. When I was a young man he would try and force himself on me repeatedly, and I would learn later that he took video footage of me through a hidden camera in the window of my room when I first moved to New Zealand. Mosaic was a place where what I had suffered was understood and could be discussed out loud, unlike the first counselling service I visited – who didn't take notes, suggested I didn't come back, and seemed generally horrified at the story I shared with them. Everyone needs a space where they can speak openly, free of judgement; I didn't know that place existed for me until Thea found Mosaic.

Thea came to support me for my first visit to Mosaic, which is situated in Wellington City, and she was welcomed. The counsellor we saw spoke with us as a couple about why I was visiting and what I had experienced. Then he asked if he might speak to Thea alone. This made me uneasy, but I obliged. This was done so he could talk frankly with Thea and learn if I was abusive toward her or displayed any further troubling behaviour of which they might need to be aware. Then I was spoken to alone, in case there was anything else I wished to share about my story that I was uncomfortable with Thea knowing. I learnt a lot about the realms of male sex abuse during that visit, including that one in six of us experience sexual abuse before the age of twenty-five, a horrifying figure. I also learnt that many of us wait decades to talk about our abuse, and by then so much damage has been done that whilst possible, recovery is so much harder than when addressed early on. My own struggles with addiction were also addressed. By this point I had well and truly moved on; but I felt lucky only to have had brushes with escapism in the form of gaming and the effects of alcohol, as opposed to a more dangerous chemical dependency that could have rapidly resulted in my death.

That visit made me aware of a community that I already belonged to but didn't know of: a community of survivors. It's not one that I have often engaged with, but it's one I belong to and am passionate about protecting. I'm not just talking about male sexual abuse survivors, but all survivors of sexual abuse; whoever you are and whatever you've been through, no matter what stage of your journey you are on, I and the rest of that community care about you.

Geographical difficulties meant that I would not visit Mosaic often, but they made sure to send me home with the name and number of someone I could talk to and trust. The most important and powerful thing I took away from Mosaic was knowing that I wasn't the only one. Whilst I wish that my fate had never befallen another soul and never would again, there is strength in knowing you are not alone.

The number Mosaic gave me was for a man named Steven, who practised psychotherapy close to my home. I reached out to him and began attending a regular Saturday meeting. Psychotherapy, or talk therapy as I prefer to call it, is a method of addressing and changing people's behaviours in order to overcome their issues. There are many different techniques and exercises utilised, and like anything else in the world it has its critics and its believers. It worked for me. What specific exercise worked? Talking; just talking about my thoughts, feelings and perceived problems with someone who could offer impartial and educated guidance without judgement was all the intervention I needed. It was liberating.

When I first met with Steven I had a good idea of what I wanted to achieve next. Thea had helped me work through the mess in my head so that I could articulate achievable outcomes. I wanted two things. First, I wanted to tell my family about what had happened to me, exposing Ernest for who he really was – but without losing my relationship with them. Secondly, I wanted justice for myself and to ensure he couldn't hurt anyone else, meaning I would need to engage with the police. Initially I was very reluctant about coming forward to the police; I was worried that I would be wasting their time, or that they might investigate my accusations and tell me I was lying. It was Thea who held my hand through that decision-making process; she guided me across the threshold of doubt and gave me the courage to do the right thing.

So I had two outcomes I wanted to achieve, but I wasn't prepared to do either. Each week Steven and I would discuss my feelings, whether I had made any progress towards my goals, and any problems I might be facing. The more Steven and I talked, the more primed I felt toward taking action. That was the most therapeutic thing for me. The more primed I became, the more tense I became with the realisation that soon I would have to put these plans into action. It wasn't going to be easy.

When Steven and I started talking about opening up to my family, I thought I would have to start by confronting Ernest. I don't think this was wrong, but in talking things through with Steven we concluded that simply confronting Ernest may not be the best way to reach my desired outcomes – in fact it might even be to their detriment. Whilst screaming at Ernest, making him understand the torture he had put me through might feel cathartic, there was also a good chance it could backfire. It would alert Ernest that I was acting against him; he would then be able to do more to protect himself, and might sow the seeds of dissension amongst my family. I wasn't going to give him that opportunity willingly. Nor did I want him knowing the police were involved; if he were still engaged in any unscrupulous activity, I wanted them to have the best opportunity to discover it before he was able to cover his tracks.

Through these sessions with Steven I also learnt to understand what I was feeling. I was still taking antidepressants, but a lower dose now – like painkillers for an injury: you don't want to be in agony, but if you can't feel anything at all you risk opening the wound again – there has to be a healthy balance.

Through discussing my pain, my concerns and the concept of blame, I came to understand that I had been blaming myself for what had happened to me. The guilt I felt for not bringing to light who Ernest was had been eating me alive. For years I had been wrestling with myself over how to process what he did to me: disconnecting from reality through the medium of online gaming, hiding behind masked personalities, manipulating people so I could feel wanted, trying to deny the abuse ever happened, drinking to forget and then finally, for a short while, fully repressing everything before it all came bubbling over again. I came to understand that he was to blame for it all. That vile creature, wearing a man's skin, had caused me all this pain. It was *his* fault. For the first time I properly allocated the blame where it belonged, with Ernest. And then it dawned on me: I hated him, not myself. Not my teachers, not my Mum, not school or the Army. I hated him with every ounce of my being. In that moment I wanted to hurt him, just as Thea had when I told her the truth.

Steven was able to talk me through it and help me rationalise my anger. I could feel all that rage now; the rage that would surface after Ernest would try and get into bed with me, that I didn't know how to direct. Now it had a purpose. I was still the same person, there was no metamorphosis or physical change, but now I had fuel and direction. I knew where to direct my hate and could clearly allocate the blame. My mind was clearer than it had ever been, and I felt a determination to see my desires to fruition for the good of everyone. That didn't make my future course any less daunting, but everything was clearer in my head now – simple, yet powerful. Soon after that session I was able to come off antidepressants entirely.

With my thoughts and emotions aligned in a singularity of disdain for Ernest, I quickly found that the constant pull to seek ways to improve myself lessened. By properly identifying my inner turmoil, I began to understand that there wasn't some secret thing I needed to know or be able to do to feel complete. My chronic sense of lack had come from not addressing my abuse. I had a plan to address it now, though, and I was just biding my time until I was ready. My life drastically improved the day I learnt who to blame and where I should be directing my hatred. Not at myself, not at anyone else – but at him.

My hatred of Ernest gave me purpose, but it didn't make the process any easier. I would still be serving my family with harrowing news. Telling Thea had been one thing; she had shown commitment to me, we loved each other, and, unlike my family, she had no loyalty to Ernest. My Mum, though – he was her husband, and I would be telling her he was a paedophile who had used me as a sexual plaything, raped me, and even photographed the aftermath. I would be telling my brothers the same thing about their father. That would shatter their perceptions of him, maybe call their entire lives into question. How would they react to that? Would they believe me? What happens if they don't? What happens if they do? They lived in a small town – what happens if word gets out? Maybe Ernest will deny any wrongdoing and I'll be wrong in their eyes. Perhaps they've known all along. These are the types of things Steven and I talked about ad nauseam. We broke down every concern I had and split it into possible outcomes ranging from likely to unlikely, discussing the potential fallout from each together with coping mechanisms. If telling my family was a long sea voyage on treacherous oceans, Steven and I slowly but surely readied my ship for the seas ahead. We talked that journey through and planned it out until there were no scenarios left to discuss, until every item I might need was aboard my ship, and every escape device loaded in the event something went wrong. Then all I had to do was set sail.

The resolution to nearly every perceived issue with telling my family was the same. It was Ernest's fault. Maybe some small-minded people would make fun of my family if they heard the news – but that was Ernest's fault. If my family did decide to question their entire lives, well then they deserve to be able to make that decision for themselves – because he did those things. The abuse I suffered was at his hands, and he was to blame for any and all fallout from it.

The first step I took towards fulfilling my goals was talking to the police. It wasn't a matter of running down to the station in a panic and demanding Ernest's arrest – not even half as dramatic as that. We called ahead of time and spoke with an officer on the phone; we told them what had happened to me, and asked how we should proceed. The process was explained thoroughly, and we were given a time the following day to come down to the station to talk things through further. We were also told the name of the officer we would be seeing. Thea and I went down together and asked to see the officer whose name we had been given. Soon he appeared and brought us through to an interview room.

At no point in the process did I feel like the police were anything but supportive. I did have concerns: that because I was making claims of abuse which were both historical and occurred overseas, my story might get picked apart and scrutinised down to the finest detail. I was worried that I wouldn't be believed. But I had discussed this scenario with Steven, and he had assured me it was unlikely.

The officer we spoke to was also careful in the way he posed his questions. It was clear that he wanted enough detail to put together a picture of what they were dealing with, but didn't want to cause me upset. I had prepared myself to go into excruciating detail, and now that I had clarity over who was to blame I could do this in a concise manner. But once I told the officer my allegations and the ages at which they had happened, he did not demand any further detail from me.

Thea and I were both concerned that once we made our claims, all parties involved would be notified and questioned. The officer handled our questions well and explained everything to us thoroughly. Ernest would not be notified until they began actively investigating him, and at that stage they would only contact my family with my permission. Essentially, unless I wanted people to find out I had made allegations, no one would – not from the police anyway. The officer explained that things could escalate if further allegations came to light, but they would inform me if that happened. The next steps were then explained: they would begin gathering available evidence (which was just my statement at this stage), contact Interpol, as this was an overseas case, and arrange for a formal video interview with me.

Something I wasn't expecting from the police that day was concern. The officer asked Thea and me if we both felt safe, or if we were concerned for my family being around Ernest; they could take action if we were, he said. But we had no reason to be worried – Ernest knew nothing, we told the officer. He still gave me a card with his direct dial and mobile numbers, and told me that if Thea or I ever felt that Ernest had become aware of us seeking justice, were anxious that he was around the house or had any concerns or questions, not to hesitate to contact him.

I had been worried prior to that initial meeting with the police that once the allegations were made, everything would be taken out of my control – that the accusations would set in motion an unstoppable sequence of events. But whilst the police made it clear that they had a duty to investigate any accusations and made no presumptions of guilt, they also assured me that I would be kept in the loop on all decisions relating to who would be called in or informed, with the caveat that if things escalated they would then act appropriately. I went to the station that day scared; I left feeling reassured and safe, like I had done the right thing. I had completed one of my goals. Now I needed to tell my family.

I continued seeing Steven each Saturday. Afterwards, Thea and I would talk through what went on at that session.

She knew I wanted to tell my family and was patiently waiting for me to be ready. If I was the captain of this voyage, she was my first mate; ultimately it was she who told me one Tuesday morning that today was the day. She knew I was ready and just needed to be pushed. We got in the car, I texted my Mum and told her we were coming, and we set off. We had set into motion a police investigation, now it was time my family was made aware of the monster who hid among us.

Thea drove, keeping us aligned to our goal. It was the job and purpose of the police to uphold the law and see that criminals be brought to justice. Whilst I never should have had to endure what I did, telling the police of Ernest's crimes was exactly what I should have done years ago. A son should never have to tell his mother that her husband is a paedophile and a rapist, but Ernest was just that. I could not allow him to deceive my family or remain hidden any longer.

Thea and I spoke the whole way to my Mum's house – it was a two-and-a-half-hour drive, so there was plenty of time to kill. I hadn't been that chatty in a long time, it's funny the effect that nervous energy has on you. We talked about work, friends, recent weekends, TV shows and holidays we'd like to take in the future, all just trying to distract ourselves from the bitter task that awaited us at the end of our journey. There was only one favourable outcome: my Mum accepting the fact that her husband was a piece of filth scraped from the underbelly of humanity. There were two other possible outcomes that worried me, the first being that she had known the whole time, the second that she wouldn't believe me. But through my sessions with Steven, I had prepared for all eventualities.

Thea and I arrived at our destination. Only I got out of the car; this was my task to complete. Thea would either join me when it was done or pick me up and drive us home, depending on the outcome. Once I shut the car door I took a moment just to be, pausing to acknowledge that just a short time ago the concept of standing here on the verge of confronting my demons would have been completely inconceivable. I hated him for making me share this news with my mother.

Though I was confident that Ernest would not be home – as an outright confrontation with him would not serve my purpose well – there would be no avoiding it if our paths crossed. Ernest had started working for the New Zealand Defence Force just before I left the Army myself. He was working, and living, in Waiouru fulltime. It was an arrangement that suited him. He was free to do whatever he wished with no one monitoring him. He would only return home on the odd weekend or for special occasions. Being a Tuesday and no one's birthday or funeral, I didn't expect that he would be there.

Mum had heard us arrive and was waiting at the door. She waved to say hello and hugged me. It had been quite some time since we had seen each other; I had been preoccupied with everything I have been describing in previous chapters – no time for social calls. She asked why Thea wasn't coming in. I could tell she was slightly on edge: turning up at short notice during the work week was not a common thing. I didn't lie to her; by the time we arrived there it was almost lunchtime, so Thea said she would drive off and get us lunch. The plan was that Thea would eat alone, but just in case things went south she would pick me up something – although I would likely not be hungry in the event that happened. So I told my Mum, "Thea is just getting some lunch, she'll probably join us later." I didn't come in guns blazing – I believe in social protocol and like to observe the pleasantries. "Should we go inside?" I suggested.

As we went inside Mum offered me a hot drink – coffee – and I could see her growing more and more uneasy. She would be an awful poker player given how obviously she displays her tells – her posture becomes more crouched, shoulders rolled forward. Just like the day she told me I couldn't see my Dad anymore. Watching her become uncomfortable was upsetting, especially as I was about to make it worse. But this was *his* fault. I was yet again reminded of how much I hated him. I asked how she had been and for news of my brothers, which helped ease the tension building in the room. We stayed on those topics until the drinks were made, at which point I suggested we move into the garden. Mum loved her garden, so I thought she would feel more at ease out there. Being in the house also reminded me of when he had made passes at me there when he thought we were alone. He wasn't worthy of being something stuck to the bottom of your shoe. We sauntered somewhat apprehensively into the garden and sat down on the bench, cautiously sipping the hot drinks we were clasping.

A few seconds passed in what felt like forever. There was no point mincing words, so I turned to my Mum and said, "I have to tell you something about Ernest – I'm not proud of how long it has taken me, but you need to know." I waited to receive an acknowledgement of my words before continuing, "He sexually abused me as a child." I had rehearsed those opening words in my head in case I got caught up or the conversation was unable to continue – if I said those words then my Mum would know who Ernest was. Fortunately the conversation continued, and I told her more, but I can't remember the exact dialogue anymore. Mum believed and accepted the news, although she wasn't comfortable that the police were involved. I called Thea and she joined us.

Thea and I would not stay much longer with my Mum; the deed we had come to do had been accomplished. Before leaving, we helped Mum book plane tickets back to England. She was going to seek support from her family, and intended to seek legal counsel. She would explain her absence to Ernest by fabricating a family emergency that she had to attend to which would keep her away for at least a month. Before we left that day, Mum and I discussed telling my brothers. I wanted to be the one to do it, and I wanted to tell them face to face and as soon as possible; they had a right to know what was going on. I do not know exactly why, but Mum asked that I wait until she returned. I didn't want to, but I agreed. All Thea and I asked of her was that under no circumstances was Ernest to be made aware that the police were involved.

Thea and I left that day having accomplished the mission we set out to complete. I felt the goals I had set, which had seemed so far away initially, were starting to be realised.

CHAPTER EIGHTEEN

Retraumatised for Retribution

WHILE I HAD no plan or intention to confront Ernest now, I had yet to break the truth to my brothers. Some degree of catharsis had come from sharing my horrible secret with my mother, though her decision to return to England so abruptly was not something I had anticipated – and did stunt my plans somewhat. Nevertheless there was a part of me that was thankful for the state of armistice her leave of absence would provide; though I had thoroughly prepared myself for telling my mother, it had still been hard.

But I was unhappy with the decision to wait a month or longer to tell my brothers. Whether it would be hard to tell them or not, they had a right to know. I was also concerned about the police investigation. Even though the police had assured me that unless extenuating circumstances arose they would contact me before reaching out to the rest of my family, I didn't know what they might uncover, and I didn't want my brothers to be blindsided – asked to make statements about their father before I had had a chance to talk with them.

My mother's departure caused me some anxiety too. She would obviously be seeking support from our wider family;

they all knew Ernest, and had their own opinions of him. I couldn't be sure that they would believe him capable of the horrors that he had subjected me to. I waited for word on how my family received the news, but I heard very little from my mother or my extended family whilst she was in the United Kingdom. They were all supportive of me and her, but I would have thanked them for relieving me from the turmoil of waiting. It's just not the type of thing people talk about. I feel it's important we change that.

I saw Steven a few more times in the coming weeks, until we both agreed that there was little more for us to discuss. He was happy for me to keep attending our sessions if I wanted; but once I was able to properly account for my emotions and allocate blame to Ernest, acknowledging and accepting what he had done to me, there was little else I needed from psychotherapy. Whilst necessary for a while, the sessions were too expensive for me to keep attending for just general counselling, as there was no financial assistance available to me. So we stopped our regular Saturday morning sessions, leaving me independent of any counselling or medication, able to stand on my own two feet with Thea's support. This was a worrying but also very affirming time for me. My wife and I had begun a chain reaction that would see Ernest's crimes brought to light, I felt affirmed that I was doing the right thing, and with the support of my wife I needed little else.

To say that the month that my Mum was away flew by would be both incorrect and accurate at the same time – almost an oxymoron. I was anxious for her return; I needed to tell my brothers about the monster their father was; I had already waited too long. There was something different about her upon her return, though. When she had left she seemed entirely concerned for me and invested in helping me; but now she seemed evasive. Communication between us was vague and sparse; whilst I don't know the extent of her thoughts, she expressed little concern for my wellbeing. I got the impression that she wanted to keep what had happened to me as quiet as possible.

Whilst I had accepted my past, telling my brothers still wasn't going to be easy. I was not responsible for what Ernest did to me or the fact that I had to share that with them, but I could sympathise with what was in store for them once they were faced with the truth, and I didn't envy them. At this point in our lives my brothers were not living in the same place anymore, and their geographical separation meant that the chances of getting them together at the same time were slim. This meant I would have to break the news to them individually – hard for them and harder for me. I would visit the elder brother first.

Thea and I made the trip to my brother's house. It was quite a distance from where we lived, and bearing bad news makes for a solemn drive. As we had done on our trip to bring my mother up to speed, we nervously chatted about everything under the sun to take our minds off our task. Mum met us there; she wanted to be able to comfort her son when he heard the news of his father. My brother welcomed us inside, always polite and happy to see family; we took off our shoes and sat on the sofas in his front room. We caught up on each other's news, omitting one item for the time being; we even laughed and joked as family do. The occasion might have been a nice one if it weren't for the grim undertaking we had to carry out. Once I felt everyone was comfortable, I told my brother I had something I needed to share with him.

You might be wondering why I didn't just lead with the news, get straight to the point as it were. Being told that your father is a twisted molester is like being stabbed in the gut. No one wants to open their front door only to be stabbed in the gut by a loved one – it's impolite, to say the least. If you're going to have your entire world spun on its head, you may as well be comfortable beforehand. There was also a lingering issue to be addressed before I could speak frankly with my brother. He lived with his partner, but my mother had pleaded with both Thea and me not to let her know what was going on. This was not in line with my wishes at all, and made me feel like I was having to keep a secret again, like I should be ashamed. Neither Thea nor I wanted this, but I agreed to it in the end. I pandered to my mother's wishes, which meant Thea had to find an excuse to take my brother's partner away from her home before I could talk with him.

Once Thea had obliged, so that it was now just me, my mother and brother at his house, it was time to do what we had come to do. My brother didn't say anything as he waited for my announcement after Thea left with his partner; he just gave me an inquisitive glance. And so I told him that his father had sexually abused me for years on end. Not in as much detail as I had gone into at my counselling sessions, or with the police – or even the vague details I had discussed with my mother. Just what he needed to know; I saw no point in burdening him with the full gravity of his father's offending. As the fact that his father was a molester crashed like a meteor into my brother's mind, I watched an avalanche of emotion cross his face. He didn't know what to say. He looked to my mother for guidance and support; she put a hand on his and they left the room. I sat and waited for their return, alone. I wondered how he would take the news; I could hear the wheel of fate spinning, deciding the outcome of this scenario. I didn't want to lose a brother.

An eternity passed in five minutes before they reappeared. I don't know what they'd spoken about. My brother said nothing as he walked up to me; he looked utterly forlorn, and agony was plastered across his face. As he kept walking towards me I wondered what his intentions were. I had decided that his reactions were his own, and that if he chose to react in an aggressive or dismissive manner then I would try to find a way to forgive him. I didn't want to lose my brother. I was preparing myself to be banished from his life and home as he came closer and closer. He leaned into his steps as if he were shifting weight to throw a punch – I braced for that impact, almost flinching; but then he embraced me. He held me as I wrapped my arms around him in return. He told me that he was sorry. That he was sorry? We sat down, and I told him he had nothing to apologise for – this wasn't his fault. There was more talk in kind before I asked him how he could so readily accept what I had shared. I was given a concerned look before he averted his gaze, telling me that as a child he would sometimes use Ernest's laptop for schoolwork. From time to time when he was doing that, he would get bored and look for games to play on it. Accidentally, in his search for games on his father's hard drive, he would come across pictures and videos of young men and boys. I could tell he was upset with himself as he continued to apologise to me. He thought his father was a closet homosexual, but he had no idea what he was doing to me. He swore if he had, he would have done something. I told my brother firmly that he had nothing to be sorry for, that none of the blame was his, and I thanked him for his support.

When I arrived at my brother's house, his perception of family had been intact: brothers, mother and father – all intact. He had only recently left university, he was working his first job, and like so many of us he was struggling to get by. But he was happy doing so, and he felt secure knowing he had support at home. But by the time I departed his house, his world had been violently shattered. He felt isolated and alone in the world, his family torn to shreds. There was no security in that. I was not the only one whose life was impacted by Ernest's crimes. Like the waves from a rock hurled into water, his disgusting acts rippled throughout our family, harming everyone they touched.

I wished the youngest of my brothers had been there in that front room. I didn't want to have to keep dragging out this arduous and heartbreaking process, and I wanted my brothers to be able to support each other as Thea supported me. I wanted as much support available for my brothers as possible, but by altering my wishes to suit my mother's I had denied him the ability to share his woe with his partner; that wasn't fair.

In hindsight, I should have waited to tell my brothers together, but I felt the urgency to make them aware. That was selfish of me, but it's how it happened, and I can't change the past. Between us we agreed that we had to break the news to my younger brother in person as soon as possible, and that we all needed to be there for him and for each other. My grandfather flew out to New Zealand from England to support my mother, as she felt she had to confront Ernest soon. My grandfather would also be in attendance when we shared the news with my younger brother.

My youngest brother had always had the closest relationship with his father and looked up to him, as sons should be able to. Though he still lived with my Mum at this point, he had recently found freedom in the form of a driver's licence, so trying to nail him down long enough to talk was hard.

It was roughly two weeks after sharing the news of Ernest's disgusting penchant for molestation and voyeurism with the elder of my two brothers before we gathered around the youngest in his room at home. I had given him no reason to believe anything was wrong; perhaps I should have managed expectations of the visit beforehand, but I felt the most respectful way to break this kind of news was entirely in person. He thought this was just a nice visit from his brothers.

I told him about his father in the same way I had my other brother. His reaction was different: he stared blankly at the wall ahead of him the entire time, and said nothing to me. I could see he was distraught and not able to process what he was hearing. I told him I was sorry – to which he didn't react – and then I took my leave, leaving my brothers to themselves. They didn't want to see me again that day. My mother hugged me, my grandfather slapped me on the shoulder whilst shaking my hand and told me that it was going to be ok. Then I left for home. I had told my family about the man Ernest was, but there was still more to be done.

My mother and grandfather had decided to confront Ernest the next week. We'd spoken about the event on the phone; I told them I wanted to be there when he was confronted, but was talked out of it – they felt that between the two of them they could manage. Though they thought they were protecting me, by letting them talk me out of being there I lost my opportunity to confront my abuser in triumph, to show him he hadn't won – to show him that I wasn't just the boy who was raped. I should have stood my ground with them, but at the time it didn't seem worth the fight; I didn't want to argue with or upset them. And I did have concerns that I might not be able to control myself and might still react with violence towards him. I convinced myself that's why I was staying away. I regret that decision, and I will likely never get another chance to show him I'm not broken. I still alerted the police of what was going on in that house, though; I was worried about things escalating out of control.

I have since been told how it all unfolded and what his reactions were. He didn't even try to deny what he had done to me, or apologise. He just walked into the lounge and sat on the sofa with his head in his hands for a short while, before asking if the police were involved. My mother told him that they were, despite Thea and I explicitly stating that we didn't want him knowing. The only emotions he displayed were out of concern for himself. And that was it – he left to spend the rest of whatever time he had dwelling in the wasteland of Waiouru, likely erasing browser histories and throwing away hard drives. Who knows what else he got up to unsupervised up there!

The next phase of the process for me was making a formal video statement for the police. I knew that it was coming – the series of events had been outlined for me during my first visit to the police station to lay a complaint about Ernest. I had lain awake at night on many occasions thinking about what I would say during the interview, and how I would say it. I knew they were going to ask me specifics, and I would need to describe some very uncomfortable situations using language that should never appear in a sentence a child is using to describe the actions of a parent. I struggled with forming a timeline, a chronological sequence of events; I knew that I had been abused on many different occasions, but there was almost too much to comb through in my brain.

One day during a lunch hour at work, the interview was on my mind. I took a refill pad and pencil, then began to note down rough times and locations in which Ernest had carried out his perverted deeds, intending to put them together in a coherent order for the police. I gave up once I reached the sixth page and realised I was nowhere near finished. I wasn't going to be able to make sense of all that he had done to me, and I don't think the people interviewing me had blocked out an entire week to work through it. He had abused me on too many occasions for me to be able to recount it all. I kept those pieces of paper to hand for the next few days, occasionally jotting down other events I would remember, and mulling over how on earth I was going to condense it all. It caused me a great deal of strife. A lot was riding on this interview: I had to be accurate and factual, something that is incredibly hard to do when you have spent years denying, repressing and trying to forget events ever happened. But I feared that if

I couldn't be concise in my accusations, that should this ever end up in court some savvy attorney would have it thrown out. Probably too much television on my behalf, mixed with a little anxiety around reliving my abuse on camera.

Eventually I decided on a course of action. When the time came, I would explain to the interviewers the first occasions when he inflicted a new form of abuse of me, as I have done in this book. I decided this because I could remember them clearly. I would explain that whilst I avoided home as much as possible, I would almost certainly be molested when I had to sleep in my own bed at home. The manner of the molestation would generally conform to the latest abuse that had been inflicted upon me. In the beginning when he was fondling me and exposing himself to me, I would be subjected to that night after night. Once the abuse had escalated further into penetration, I would endure that every night.

The New Zealand Police would be providing my video interview to Interpol, so England was the focus of what I would talk about; but I made sure to explain the details of my arrival in New Zealand and his continued advances once I had made it here. Whilst I had not allowed him to take advantage of me after we parted ways the first time in England, I thought it pertinent to make them aware that he did not stop pursuing me. I thought his unsuccessful advances were all that happened in New Zealand. My Mum would later tell me of his sickening behaviour behind the blind with the gap, when I would send him away from my room.

Before I conducted my video interview, my mother and the older of my two brothers had been asked to provide statements to the police in regard to the allegations I was making. My younger brother had not witnessed anything, and if he had he would have been too young to comprehend it. I knew that this was being asked of them, but I did not ask for any details of their statements – whilst I was curious, I felt it would be disrespectful. If they wanted to share what they would write with me, that was up to them.

My mother wanted to share some details with me; we had discussed details of my abuse already, and were able to confirm dates and places in which certain events occurred. Previously we had only talked briefly about Ernest's actions after I rejoined the family in Aotearoa; whilst I had divulged to my mother that he had made advances toward me when he thought everyone else was asleep, she had not yet shared anything with me from that time. Now she told me of a day when Ernest had gone to work without his cell phone. He had left it on the kitchen counter forgetfully, and she had decided to go through it – as people do, I suppose. Whilst it was an older phone without much connectivity, it did have both video and camera capabilities. When perusing that phone she found footage and photos of me taken from behind that blind in my room. I would ignore Ernest spying on me from behind it when I denied his passes at me because it was easier than confronting him. That blind. He had videoed and photographed me, not just when I sent him away and knew he was watching, but during the day, when I got out the shower, when I got changed – he had documented almost everything I had ever done in that room and kept it for his own purposes.

I felt sick to my stomach, and completely let down by my mother. She apologised profusely, and I have accepted her apology on the grounds that she found nothing too sinister when looking through the phone. But it's still hard for me to reconcile this event: what she found on his phone and her ensuing action – the action of doing nothing. Ernest had manipulated us all.

The day came for my video interview. I was given the time and place where I should be, an inconspicuous building in Petone. The Officer in charge of my case met me there, explained again what would be happening, and assured me I need not worry. The Officer was there to witness the things I would say and ensure that I presented enough detail during the interview for a conviction to be sought. The interview played out exactly as had been explained to me, and the facilitators were incredibly supportive – if I didn't know that I was there to be recorded, I wouldn't have known it was happening. Thea accompanied me that day, but did not come into the interview room.

The interview room was comfortable, and there were facilities for breaks as well. The building was well lit and colourful on the inside. When you are having to relive abuse, be retraumatised, it makes a huge difference if you can do it in friendly and comfortable surroundings. The interviewers had the statement I had already made to the police and were further briefed on my situation; they then spent time beforehand talking with me, getting to know me. Once I was ready, we started. I began by elaborating further on my statement, then moved onto what I had planned out with my timeline of events. A best-effort attempt at a chronological ordering of the escalating events comprising the sexual abuse I suffered.

If I could offer anyone any advice for these interviews, it would be to plan out what you are going to say, write it down, and be prepared to go into graphic detail. I described the events of my abuse much as I have in this book. When talking about the occasion in Spain where he had me give him a blowjob, I had to be specific. I had to say the words, "My stepfather Ernest made me get on my knees, open my mouth and allow him to put his penis inside. He then demanded that I suck." When describing how he penetrated me for the first time, I had to tell them how he told me to lie down face first and hold my butt cheeks open as he took his unlubricated penis and penetrated my anus; and I had to tell them my age, who else I had been with, and the time of day. That is the detail you must be prepared to give. It was traumatising but necessary, and having a plan written down will help the process.

Each time we discussed an event the facilitators made sure I was ok, and reminded me we could stop at any time. They put no pressure on me to hurry up. I drew floor plans of the rooms I was abused in, told them about the family members who knew of my whereabouts at times of abuse – and they wanted to know all about my school and tutors who were in my company regularly. No stone was left unturned. I had expected to feel mortified when it was finished. I didn't – I felt nervous, but also a sense of tremendous release. I had delved a lot deeper into my memories of abuse that day, but I hadn't done it for nothing. Between this interview and the statements provided by my family, the police had everything necessary for them to build a case against Ernest. He would soon answer for his crimes.

CHAPTER NINETEEN

Terminus

WITH EACH STEP toward retribution and seeing Ernest brought to justice I felt better in myself, as if I had been trapped in the shadows, but was now slowly stepping out into the sunlight. The police in New Zealand had all they needed from me, and most of my family were now aware of the man Ernest was, this man who had been the scourge of my existence for over a decade.

My quality and enjoyment of life drastically improved as a result. I felt more confident with each passing day: I could look people in the eye when we spoke, hold my ground and be assertive in situations I would have previously attempted to evade. I could talk about myself in a positive manner, without feeling like I was wasting the time of whomever I was conversing with. These developments were huge leaps and incredible successes in their own right, but they weren't the only benefits that shedding the burden of secrecy were bringing. By coming forward and being open about my abuse, by no longer repressing or denying the memories and allowing them to settle in their rightful place – the past – they stopped haunting me. I found I had infinitely more bandwidth in my thoughts; I would recall the lessons I had been trying to learn during my obsessive self-improvement period. It had been a mindless obsession fuelled by neurosis and compulsion; but now I was able to recall some of that learning and put it to good use. As a result I even successfully applied for a promotion at work (something I would definitely have not felt worthy of in years past), impressing my employer with my knowledge of workplace psychology, methods of implementing positive philosophies in the workplace as a tool for engagement, and management styles. All things I had known for a long time, but buried and unreachable in a mind plagued by darkness.

After joining the Army I would sometimes think of returning to England. He was no longer there, so I should have been able to perceive it as a safe place, but I couldn't. I associated it with my abuse; even the idea of returning there for a short time filled me with dread. I had sworn to myself I wouldn't return, and for a long time I didn't. But after shedding the shackles that his abuse had wrapped around my life, I began to view England in a far more positive light. I even started to want to go back and see family there. I no longer associated England with my abuse; I now knew exactly where and with whom the blame lay. My wife had not met my biological father or any of his side of the family. We were able to rectify that in late 2018 when we returned to England together, a wonderful trip spent surrounded by family – something I thought that I would never be able to do.

During our trip I met with the police officer handling my case against Ernest in England. There were no major developments in the case besides what myself and my family had provided in evidence. Ernest had indicated that he intended to cooperate and plead guilty, depending on what he was charged with. At the time I was surprised by this news.

The last task I had to undertake on our trip was to tell my Dad and his family of my abuse. I had completely come to terms with it by this point – it was a chapter in my life that I had moved on from and accepted. That didn't make it any easier to tell my Dad about it; there was no way he wouldn't feel guilty for the circumstances under which he was prevented from seeing me. I made sure to tell him that I did not blame him in any way, that there was no way he could have known. I had struggled to maintain a relationship with him even after he reached out to me when I was eighteen. But the positive side of sharing my story with him is that we are now closer than we have ever been.

Back in New Zealand, my mother and brothers had to settle into their lives after a period of extreme unrest, now without Ernest. After coming forward I had begun to experience hugely beneficial changes, but theirs has been a more solemn story. They had chosen the red pill – they accepted the harsh reality which I presented to them, that the man they knew was in fact a sex offender and molester. My mother and younger brother found it especially difficult to adjust now. They had lost their husband and father respectively, and his income. This resulted in having to sell their home and find somewhere else to live.

In early 2019 the UK Crown Prosecution Service decided to proceed with Ernest's prosecution. A summons was issued, and a warrant put out for his arrest. To avoid extradition, Ernest voluntarily made his own way to England. My mother made me aware of his movements and I contacted the police in England, who arrested him as he entered the country. They charged him with fifteen varying accounts of sexual abuse against a minor. Once charged, he again indicated he would plead guilty to them all. Was this some kind of conscientious decision to seek penance for his sins? Perhaps he felt remorse or guilt, and now sought absolution. Whilst I can't speak for him, personally I doubt it.

Since leaving the Army in the UK he had always sought out jobs where he would be able to work with young men who needed assistance with their literacy and numeracy – vulnerable young men. I am merely speculating, based on my own experiences, when I say that he more than likely tried to worm his way into at least one of these young men's beds. Then there was also the question of his online activity. I am confident that he did not keep all the images he took of me to himself; I am not that naïve. I imagine they were likely traded with other members of his sick community for some of the content my brother would stumble across when he was supposed to be doing homework on his father's laptop. So no, I don't believe he was seeking atonement, but rather an easy way out. By pleading guilty to the crimes I had accused him of and in the face of testimony from his family, he would avoid a trial and any further prying into his unscrupulous activities, thus negating the chance of any further charges being laid. And in the United Kingdom, as I'm sure Ernest would have been well aware, when charged with a crime and pleading guilty in the first instance, any sentence passed down is automatically reduced by a third.

I suffered because of him. Suffered every day, for over a decade, inside the violent echo chamber of my mind. I endured abuse, addiction and poor mental health, resulting in a multitude of other issues – all because of his actions. I tried my best to repair the damage he did to me and to make something of myself; a formidable challenge that I would have failed without the love and support of my wife, Thea. I had to expose my family to a terrible hurt and burden my wife with more than it would have been fair for her to shoulder in a hundred lifetimes. But for all of that, justice was served in late 2019: my stepfather was sentenced to twelve years in prison. Because of his cooperation he will serve a maximum of eight years behind bars. In reality, he will likely serve much less, as the criminal justice system considers him to be "of good character". It is unnerving how someone convicted of sex crimes against a child can be considered to be cooperative and of good character.

But regardless of my opinion on the matter, it's not for me to say whether or not his sentence was fair. When I first considered taking the matter of my abuse to the police, I could not imagine making it this far. I thought at best my allegations would serve as a red flag or a warning of his presence; that if any other, more recent claims of offending were to arise, then my allegations would add weight to them. I had not expected the testimony of my family to be so damning of him, nor the New Zealand Police to take a historical, overseas case so seriously.

Have the scales of justice been balanced? I don't know, and I'm unwilling to debate it. What I can tell you is this: I am immensely proud of Thea; we now have a renewed outlook and appreciation for life, free of his pestilent presence. I could not have achieved any of what I have done without her

– she has been my rock and my guiding star throughout this laborious process. Everything that I have achieved during this process I owe to her.

I am proud of how far my family have come on this journey in the face of adversity. The elder of my brothers, in particular, showed incredible courage at a time when it would have been far easier for him to turn a blind eye, instead choosing to support me and add his voice to my cause against his father. I couldn't be more proud of him or grateful for his actions.

My family believed me and bolstered my claims with their own statements; this greatly aided me in the pursuit of justice. As a victim of sexual abuse, however, I needed more than that. I needed emotional support and reassurance that I was doing the right thing, something that I did not get. There were times when I would receive a message from a family member causing me to call into question my motives and making me feel that perhaps I was being selfish, or that I should try and retract my allegations to the police. In such times it was Thea who stepped in to keep me on track. There were times when members of my family were clearly struggling to come to terms with what Ernest had done, which caused them a great deal of strife; that much is understandable. What is not ok is how those feelings of strife were then projected onto me. I was lumped with their feelings of turmoil, and at times made to feel responsible for their sorrow. I had to act as a support person for them; had I not had Thea in my corner, that would have been enough to make me give up. Had I pandered to what my family wanted of me, Ernest would likely still be a free man.

I will be forever grateful to both the New Zealand and British police forces for the respect they showed me and the diligence with which they pursued my accusations. Through the actions of my family and the police, we have been able to cut out my stepfather's infectious presence, and our lives will be better for it. I have grown closer with my family all over the globe.

With his sentencing came security – he is no longer a free man, and cannot harm anyone else. But the most momentous thing his sentencing brought about for me was closure; and had I not had Thea by my side, I most likely would never have found that completion.

CHAPTER TWENTY

Hatred Well Applied

THAT'S WHERE MY story of abuse ends. With the end of this book imminent, I would like to reflect on a part of coming forward about abuse that is particularly hard to navigate and manage: the behaviours and emotional states of others. I have purposely left this aspect out, for the most part, because this is my story, told from my perspective. In the interest of transparency, though, it needs some discussion.

Talking about other people's feelings is a tumultuous topic, a veritable minefield of upset. When approaching this chapter I was entirely unsure how to write it, so I took some advice from Mark Twain: "When in doubt, be truthful." I am going to tell you, honestly, how I perceived my family members' reactions, and how they made me feel. If I am wrong, let it be so.

I was the victim in this story, *I* was the one who was abused; but I found myself having to balance the emotional needs and desires of others against my own. What Ernest did rocked my family to its core; but he did those things to *me*. His actions rippled out and splashed against others, but I bore the impact of the tsunami. No survivor should ever have to listen to someone else paint themselves as the victim in their story of abuse, or put aside their own wishes for recovery to facilitate someone else's. I had to endure that, and it was unfair. Thea was left to pick up the pieces when I was left broken by that behaviour.

I was asked to keep my story a secret when all I wanted to do was be honest with people, and at times I had the reins pulled from my grasp in my own case with the police. I should have been the centre of my family's concerns during this case, but I wasn't; I was made to feel separate. I felt that my Mum and brothers were on their journey and Thea and I were on ours, in separate vehicles travelling to the same destination.

There is no script available, no how-to guide on how to behave when you learn that a family member has been sexually abused – and of course, no one should ever have to be told that in the first place. Each individual will act in his or her own way when faced with a terrible situation, but the most important thing that survivors of abuse need is support. There is an important distinction to be made between belief and support: my family believed me, but they did not support me. Thea is the one who supported me and gave me what I needed; she was the one who helped share the load, told me everything was going to be ok, and helped me through the tough times.

Belief is simply accepting that something is true, not denying that it happened, and being honest when asked about it. Support is so much more than that – it's belief, acceptance, compassion, love and commitment to help someone through their struggles, not adding to the already crushing weight they bear. I wanted to feel closer to my family, to feel like they had rallied behind me against Ernest. But instead I felt as if I was dragging them along with me. I expended a lot of effort in my concern for my family and their wellbeing; I would do it again because I love them – but I should have been allowed to focus on myself. I should have felt I had their support behind me, and been able to draw strength from that. Instead, I felt my energy being sapped.

If I can offer anyone in a position to support a survivor advice, it would be to do so wholeheartedly. If you aren't completely committed to their recovery, then get out of the way because you are going to hold them back. Be present, listen and understand what they want, don't colour their goals with your own perceptions of what should happen. Be honest; if you want to offer advice then do so plainly, but be prepared to let it go. Let them know that you support them, but more importantly back it up with action; be specific with your intentions, don't offer vague sentiments of support. Tell them exactly how and when you can help. Survivors don't have spare mental capacity to worry about organising other people or things they need help with, but even the smallest gesture can help. Are they struggling to keep up with housework or errands? Offering to assist with those tasks is simple, but will be huge. Perhaps they're yearning for social interaction – set a date and time to hang out. Don't say, "Let's hang out some time," say, "Let's hang out tomorrow at five down at the café." Let them know you're invested and you care. It will make the world of difference.

There's also an important emotional component to supporting a survivor, no matter how close you are to them. Trust me when I say they have battled with feelings of guilt, shame, fear and self-loathing; they don't need anyone else piling onto that. Don't ever try and explain their abuser's action, even with the best of intentions; it won't help them. Don't project your negative feelings onto them: cases of sexual abuse make everyone feel rubbish, but it's up to you to be strong for them. Don't add to their concerns; is someone you know close to the case also reacting badly? That's unfortunate; but if you tell the survivor that, even though it's not their fault, they're going to blame themselves, and that isn't fair. Each person's reaction is their own to manage, they are not the survivor's responsibility; don't make it their problem.

All of that is obviously based on my own experience, which may imply that I hold my family in contempt for their behaviour. I certainly did for a time, but I don't now. I would have liked them to have behaved in a more supportive manner – it would have been better for me, and saved Thea a lot of pain – but no one can dictate the actions of others. Ultimately, the cause of all this was Ernest. He is to blame for all the strife I encountered, and he is the only one I hold in contempt. Any hurt or upset caused by something someone did or didn't do after the abuse can be laid at his feet, and I hate him for it.

I have made peace with the terrible fate I suffered. My experience did not break me, but my perception of the world will always be coloured by what Ernest did to me. Given closure, I am in a position to healthily manage my outlook on life. I released my demons from their cell and confronted them, though not alone. After years of keeping them locked away in the confines of my mind, where they would wreak havoc and spread trepidation throughout my life, they have now been banished entirely.

You may naturally pose the question to me, "Why do you talk about hate so much, then?" 'Hate' and 'anger', as many of us have come to understand the words, imply some kind of lingering, unresolved issues that need addressing. Yet these feelings are not still more demons lurking in the darkness, but natural reactions – they are emotions that we all feel. There are negative connotations associated with the words, yes, but I would argue those connotations are largely false. It is true that if you choose to suppress these feelings when they bubble up inside you rather than exercise them in a healthy manner, they can fester and mutate over time into hostility and resentment. But anger and hate can be powerful and healthy forces if exercised in a constructive manner.

Rather than entombing your anger and hate where they can decompose and toxify, choose to use them as motivators for positive change. Feelings of anger are stirred within us in response to wrongdoing and injustice. These emotions are not synonymous with acts of physical aggression, as they have colloquially become known, and can be used as momentum for peaceful reconciliation. There have been times in all our lives where we have acted with irrational anger only to regret the consequences – to err is to be human. But if you truly understand the source of your hate, then you can focus it in a calm manner. When people lash out in impassioned acts of rage it's because they lack a well-defined goal, and they have no vision for the future that they would see fulfilled. That is not how I would see my anger utilised.

I hate sexual abuse and its effects, yet I am not flailing

blindly trying to harm my assailants. Instead I am channelling that hate into sharing my story, through which I hope to affect change for the better. I have grasped my anger tightly and manipulated it to see my will made manifest without violence or resentment. My hatred is a source of positivity and healing. I am angry that I was sexually abused and I hate the fact that sexual abuse is still happening; my heart breaks for each and every victim of sexual abuse and their families. Anything less passionate than hate could serve no purpose.

I would see sexual abuse annihilated, eradicated from our society, not through violence but through education and conversation. In order to protect those who may fall victim to sexual abuse in the future, we must lift the stigma around talking about it. That is what hate has done for me: it has instilled in me sufficient passion and purpose to stand up and say "I am a survivor of sexual abuse," and not be fearful or embarrassed about the repercussions of judgement. Every person who hears or sees me sharing my personal experiences is another person who knows that they have support for sharing theirs. There is strength in unity, and there are a lot of us out there.

Every time you share a story of abuse, the light shines a little brighter into the darkness where those abhorrent predators await their prey. If we all shared our stories, the light would be so blinding that they would have no place to conceal themselves. Those predators who carry out these despicable crimes hunt the ignorant and the innocent alike, wearing the silence and stigma surrounding sexual abuse like a cloak to disguise themselves. If you hate sexual abuse, like I do, then I would encourage you to talk about it; let us be rid of this stigma for good.

Never again will I apologise for a sex offender as the voices in my head apologised for my stepfather. Never. My thoughts are only with helping the victims and ending the scourge. But in order to do that we have to discuss rehabilitation for the perpetrators.

A voice in my mind once made excuses for my stepfather's actions, telling me he was unwell. Though there was no excuse for his actions, that voice was right in a sense. Whether he was unwell or not, he needed help. Once he molested me it was too late for him – perhaps he will have a chance of rehabilitation one day, but the damage has already been done. He will always be a child molester now, and nothing will ever change that. Yet there are still those out there struggling with whatever disembodied hellion is driving them towards sexually abusing another human being, and there is still hope for them to quash it. By lifting the stigma we open avenues for these people to seek help before they act on their impulses. We must encourage education and treatment, so that no more abusers enter this world.

I hate sexual abuse and will continue to take action to end its presence in society. The reach of my influence is limited, but if even one person feels empowered by this book to reach out to a friend, talk openly about abuse, or act against an abuser, then I will consider it a success.

I have shared my story of abuse and my associated struggles to shine a light into the abyss, hoping you will see my beacon and add your torch to mine. Each time a voice is added to the conversation around sexual abuse the stigma is reduced, and our torches will shine brighter still. I hope to one day live in a world where no one will ever have to endure what I did, and I call upon you to help me achieve that. You have read my story of hate and acceptance; now I call on you to spread my message and yours, to help me bring an end to the scourge that is sexual abuse.

Buried Alive – Recommended Resources

At points in my story I mentioned services I accessed to assist me in my recovery, and how hard Thea had to work to find them. I hope that anyone reading my story is inspired to seek help, wherever you may be; asking for help is not a sign of weakness, but a display of determination to remain strong.

My journey toward recovery took place in New Zealand, and so I can only recommend New Zealand-based resources. Here are some details of services that will be able to assist and guide you, no matter where you are in New Zealand.

1) If you or someone else needs immediate help – **call the Police** on 111.

2) **Mosaic** was an invaluable resource to me – the people there are passionate about helping survivors. Their mission: "To support male survivors of trauma and sexual abuse to empower themselves through education, and access to services that facilitate their healing."

Mosaic operates throughout the Greater Wellington region, but can be contacted by Skype, phone or email by survivors and their loved ones throughout New Zealand.

Find out more at: *https://www.mosaic-wgtn.org.nz/*

3) Another great resource I have come across since writing this book is **safetotalk.nz**. They are a service set up by the New Zealand Government to put those of us who have or may have experienced sexual harm in contact with trained specialists. These are some of the ways they may be able to help you:

· They provide contact with a trained specialist at any time, day or night, seven days a week
· Answers to questions about sexual harm
· Information about medical, emotional, and behavioural issues related to harmful experiences
· Explanations of what you might expect if you report to the Police
· Referral to specialists in your area
· Information for family and friends wanting to help someone
· Information, and contact with a specialist, for people who are worried about their own sexually harmful thoughts or behaviour.

Find out more at: *https://www.safetotalk.nz/*

Follow the author of *Buried Alive: A story of hate and acceptance* on Twitter at *https://twitter.com/AlexJamesInc*

Printed in Great Britain
by Amazon

41470607R00124